Gene Davis: Drawings

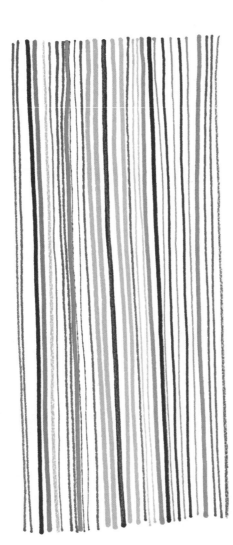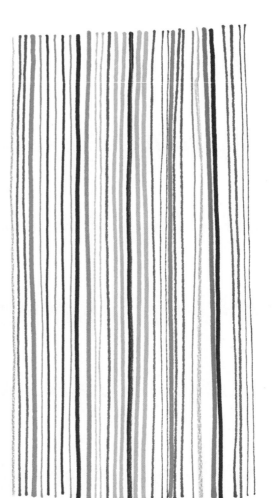

GENE DAVIS
DRAWINGS

Introduction by Gene Baro

THE ARTS PUBLISHER, INC., NEW YORK

FRONTISPIECE
King's Gate. *1981. Magic Marker.*
12½ x 18". Private collection

Unless otherwise noted, all drawings are collection the artist.

Library of Congress Catalogue Card No. 82-74159
ISBN: 0-939742-04-7

Design: Patrick Cunningham

First Edition

© The Arts Publisher, Inc., 1982

The Arts Publisher, Inc., New York

Printed and bound in the United States of America

Gene Davis: 30 Years of Drawing

Drawing begins with a mark on a support surface. The most sublime masterpieces develop from this apparently casual act of the artist. The tool or tools will be important in giving variety and precision to the emerging concept. The absence or presence of color will confer its individual discipline. But it is the mark, after all, the characteristic turn and pressure of pencil or pen, crayon or charcoal, pastel stick or brush, on which the drawing depends.

The drawing's energy is the mark's essence. Through the means of more or less, the artist creates space on the neutral sheet, establishes image and mood, declares presence. And almost more important than these, he communicates a special way of seeing that is at the heart of artistic personality.

For some artists drawing is a preparatory stage for painting or sculpture. For others it may be an obsession—the endless struggle for a theoretical graphic perfection. For others still, it is an activity as natural as breathing. Or else, no less natural, it may be intermit-

tent. A period of drawing intensively is not uncommon among painters and sculptors—drawing for its own sake taking over and releasing the artist temporarily from other concerns. But, also, there are painters and sculptors who draw freely concurrently with the creation of work in their principal medium. The drawing impulse takes many forms, governed by personal needs and sometimes subject to external influence and stimulus.

Gene Davis, for instance, began to draw seriously in the early 1950's. He was painting already, but his drawings of the time were especially sensitive to the idiom developed by Arshile Gorky. Davis worked in India ink, with occasional additives of wash, to produce a parallel language to that of the admired master. Sexual imagery was abstracted, and biomorphic forms served both structural and expressive ends.

It's fair to say that Davis' drawings over the balance of the decade continued to deal with influences out of art history or out

5

of the immediate contemporary scene. The sources, sometimes directly referential, were also diverse in approach and attitude. Davis overcame his lack of academic training by fixing his imagination on what he valued and admired. He honed his skills, not for the purpose of imitation, but so as to reinvent for himself and to put to his personal uses the potent images that moved him.

Between 1955 and 1957, he produced many drawings in a realistic mode. Rembrandt's drawings were a primary source. Davis would sometimes quote the work of the seventeenth-century Dutch master. In a number of instances, he drew variations of well-known Rembrandt images and themes. The style of this work was loose, even improvisatory. Davis retained India ink as his principal vehicle though his use of wash increased substantially at this time.

Picasso and Klee were other sources for Davis' drawings of the period, particularly the former. There is evidence of growing firmness in Davis' handling of the heads and figures inspired by Picasso's work. But with all of his appreciation and apparent dependence upon other artists, it becomes increasingly clear that Davis worked consistently toward the achievement of a personal style. These many significant encounters were essentially a means to self-examination, a rigorous testing of himself.

In the late 1950's, Davis turned to collage under the brief and superficial influence of Rauschenberg and Johns. It was a time when Davis developed his own scale, more intimate and personal than what was developing in the Pop Art idiom. Social commentary in Davis' collages was idiosyncratic. These works released a playfulness in the artist, an appreciation in naiveté, a child-like quality that has persisted with various force in his drawings of the 70's and 80's.

Davis worked both on paper and masonite. He depended to some extent on found images, usually from popular periodicals or nudist magazines. Scribbled pencil lines and strokes of crayon enliven these images, providing a gloss of the artist's reactions and inviting the viewer to deal with these materials with a like imaginative spontaneity. This body of work executed in 1958 is remarkable in that it retains its freshness today. It is as if the artist had penetrated to a level of joyfulness that lay outside temporal concerns.

During the 1960's, Davis' artistic emphasis shifted to painting. A few colored ink drawings done in 1965 are all that Davis produced during the decade. This was the period of intensive development of his stripe paintings with their single-minded examination of the rhythms of color interval and other important questions of color relationship. As Davis has said, "Drawing seemed temporarily irrelevant."

But what of the drawings of 1965? These are unlike anything else Davis had tried. They depend upon perspective renderings of geometric shapes in bright colors. Some connection can be found between these drawings and his micro-paintings that date from 1966.

Mainly between 1972 and 1974, Davis turned his attention to stripe drawings. The general concerns of the paintings were translated to paper. Davis now worked with colored pencils. He used muted pale colors in clusters, achieving images of shimmering subtlety. This was in contrast to the stripe paintings which tended to be bright and aggressive in coloration. These drawings certainly enlarged Davis' visual vocabulary, particularly where color nuance was concerned. Over the years he has continued to do stripe drawings. These are sometimes done free-hand and have therefore an improvisational feeling. More formal treatments were achieved with magic marker.

The 1970's proved a most fertile period for Davis' drawings. Not only did he do more work, but he drew with a steadily enlarging sense of freedom. The variety is noteworthy. In a sense,

7

Davis returned to his collages of 1958 for inspiration. After the rigorous discipline of painting the hard-edge stripes of the 1960's, no doubt he felt the need to give full vent to the abundant energy and playfulness of his vision. In the drawings of the 1970's, there is a loosening of technique that opens the images to imagination. The vocabulary is for the most part abstract though with some superimposition of realistic images. The mixtures of vivid images call upon many kinds of marks and tools to impose their particular sense of freedom. The drawings of the 1970's are at once child-like and sophisticated, humorous, unrestrained, but nevertheless sensitive to graphic structure and formality.

The opening years of the 1980's have seen a continued outpouring of drawing from Davis. The work has become consistently more expressive, a real distance from the lyrical impressionistic stripe drawings of the early 70's. Once again, the artist has returned to collage. In these recent years, he has also executed a group of drawings in India ink with quill pen that are notably loose in handling. Sexual images, too, have returned to the work. Stylistic and technical broadness, a searching restlessness prevail in these opening years of the decade.

Perhaps no artist is more responsive to or at least more curious about the developing art scene. In his drawings, Davis reacts to the various directions temporarily prevalent in the art world but maintains through all his bright activity and empathy an unerring sense of himself. Certainly few artists have managed to talk with drawing as he has, making a dialogue so clearly his own.

Gene Baro

PLATES

1. Inner Space. *1952. Ink and wash. 13½ × 16½"*

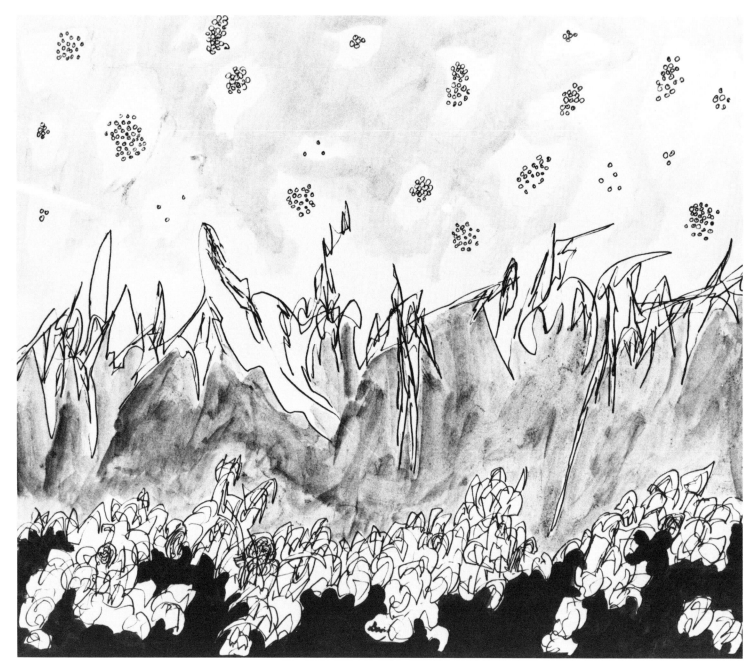

2. Seascape. 1952. Ink and wash. 13½ × 16½"

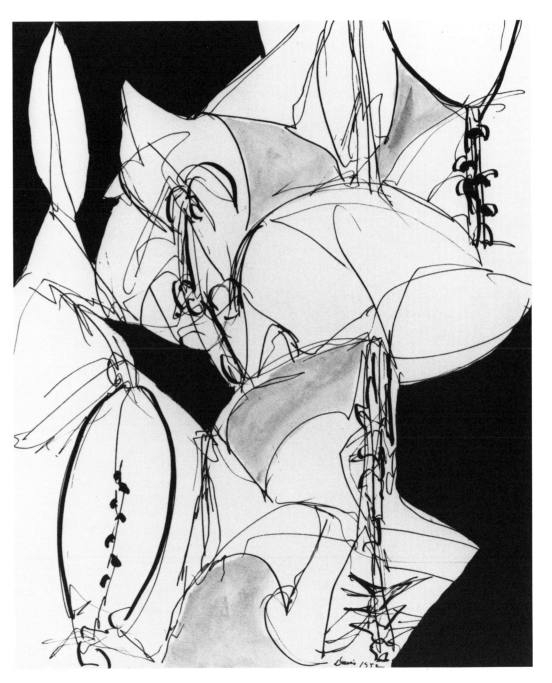

3. Secret Garden. 1952. Ink and wash. 16⅜ × 13½"

4. Sky Machine. *1952. Ink. 17¾ × 23½″*

5. Homage to Arshile. *1952. Ink and wash. 13 × 17"*

6. Mine Field. *1952. Ink and wash. 13⅞ × 16¾"*

7. Visitation. *1952. Ink and wash. 13½ × 16½".*
Hirshhorn Museum and Sculpture Garden, Smithsonian Institution, Washington, D.C.

8. Saber Dance. 1952. Ink and wash. 13½ × 16½″

9. *Queen Bee. 1952. Ink and wash. 13⅞ × 16¾″*

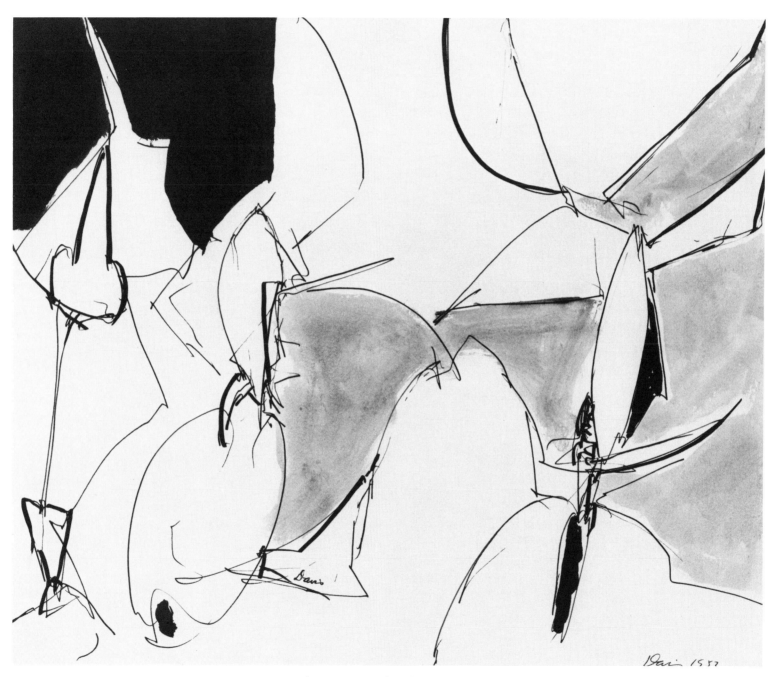

10. Parachute. *1952. Ink and wash. 13½ × 16½″*

11. Scooter. 1952. Ink and wash. 23½ × 17¾"

12. Angel Vine. *1952. Ink and wash.* 16⅜ × 13½″

13. Tin Drum. *1952. Ink and wash. 13½ × 16½".*
Hirshhorn Museum and Sculpture Garden, Smithsonian Institution, Washington, D.C.

14. Leap Frog. *1952. Ink and wash.* 13½ × 16½"

15. Midnight Garden. *1952. Ink and wash. 16¾ × 13¾"*

16. Evil Flowers. *1952. Ink and wash. 16¾ × 13¾"*

17. Signs. *1952. Ink and wash. 16¾ × 13¾"*

18. Bird Land. *1952. Ink and wash. 16¾ × 13¾"*

19. Typhoon. 1952. Ink and wash. 13⅞ × 16¾"

20. Angel Dust. *1952. Ink and wash. 16¾ × 13⅞"*

21. Volley Ball. *1955. 16³⁄₈ × 13⁵⁄₈″*

22. Man Thumbing His Nose. *1955. 16¼ × 13¼″*

23. Man at the Pump. *1955. 16¼ × 13⅝″*

24. Monument to Crows. *1956. Pencil and watercolor. 8½ × 11″*

25. Two Crosses. 1956. Pencil and watercolor. 8½ × 11″

26. Crazy Triangle. *1956. Pencil and watercolor. 8½ × 11″*

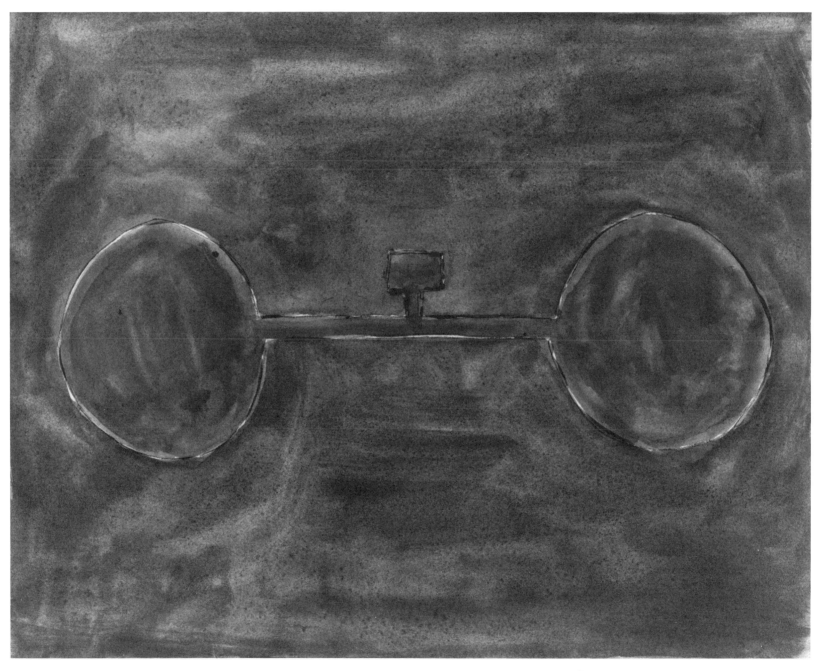

27. Devil's Wagon. *1956*. *Pencil and watercolor. 8½ × 11″*

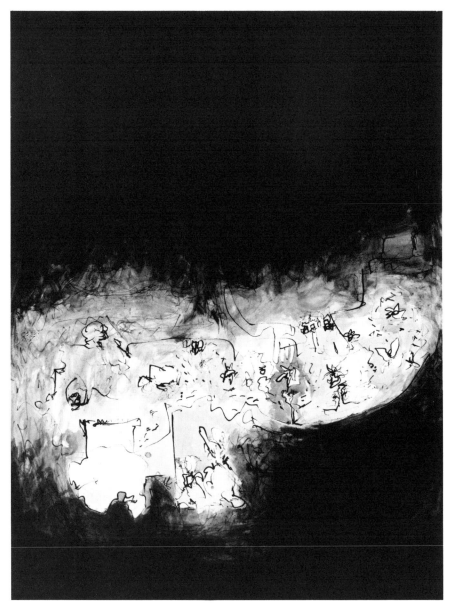

28. Garden of Evil. 1957. Ink and wash. 40 × 30"   *29. Night Demons. 1957. Ink and wash. 29¾ × 22"*

30. Black Mass. *1957. Ink and wash. 17³/₄ × 23¹/₂"*

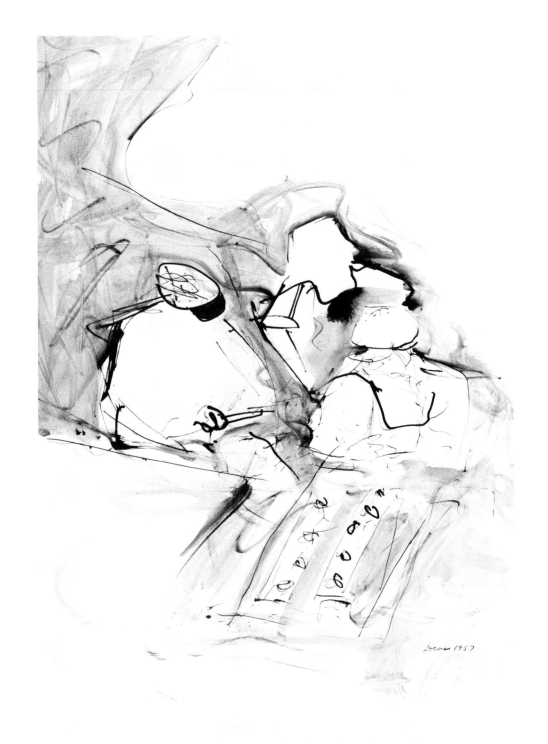

31. Even Trade. 1957. Ink and wash. 23½ × 17¾"

32. Under Flowers. 1957. Ink and wash. 23½ × 17¾"

33. Toad Stool. *1957. Ink and wash. 23½ × 17¾"*

34. Dancer. *1957. Ink and wash. 23½ × 17¾"*   35. Hot Message. *1957. Ink and wash. 16½ × 13¾"*

36. Conversation. 1957. Ink and wash. 23½ × 17¾"

37. *Clown. 1957. Ink and wash. 23½ × 17¾"*

38. Homage to Rembrandt. *1957. Ink and wash. 23½ × 17¾"*

39. Night Cap. *1957. Ink and wash. 23½ × 17¾"*

40. Woman and Ball. *1957. Ink and wash. 23½ × 17¾"*

41. Boob Tube. *1956. Ink and wash. 16½ × 13¾"*

42. Vortex. 1957. Ink and wash. 23⅝ × 17¾"

43. *Voyeur. 1957. Ink and wash.* 23½ × 17¾″

44. Keeping Score. *1957. Ink and wash. 16½ × 13¾"*

45. Inner Circle. *1957. Ink and wash. 16½ × 13¾"*

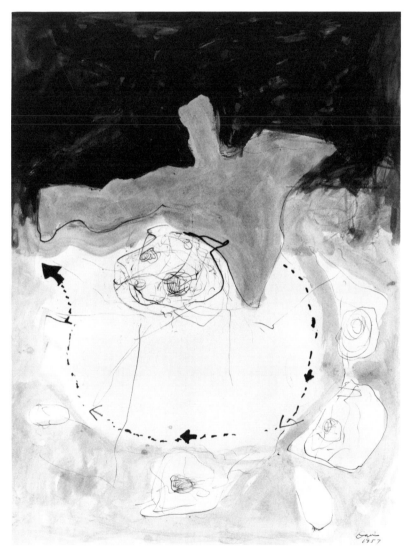

46. Night Flight. *1957. Ink and wash. 23½ × 17¾"*

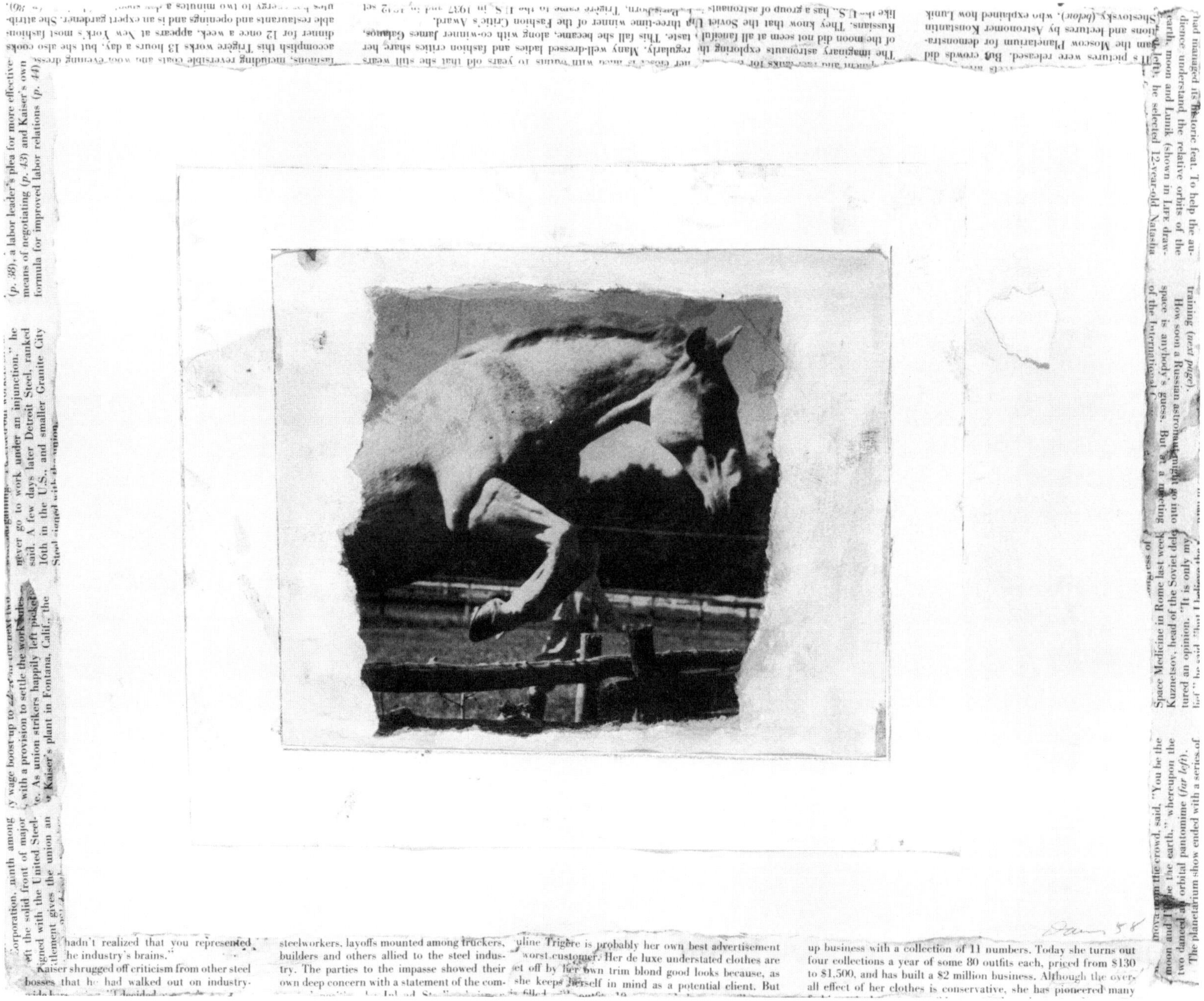

47. Leaping Horse. *1958. Collage. 11¼ × 14⅜"*

49

48. Head Stand. *1958. Collage. 11¼ × 14⅜″*
Collection Andrew Crispo, New York

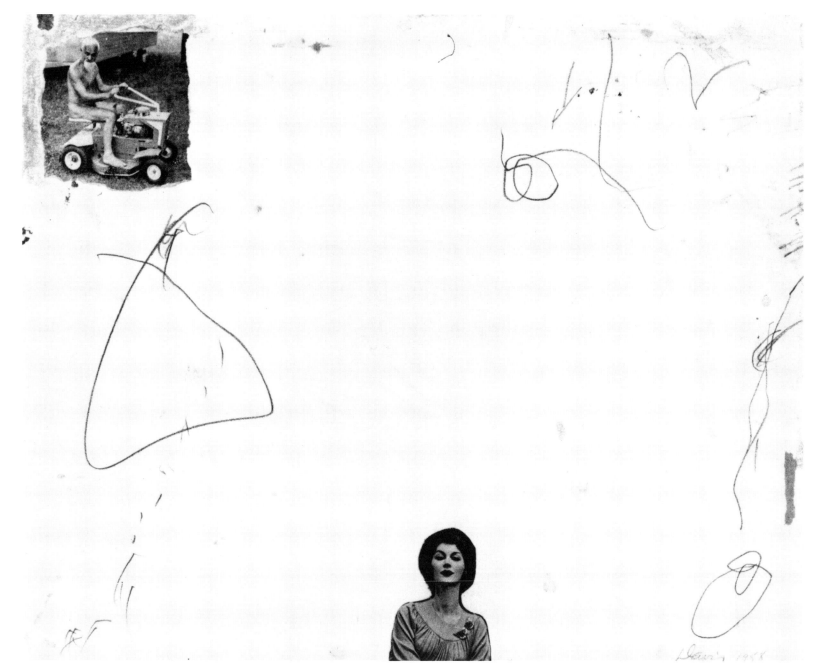

49. Lawn Mower. *1958. Collage. 11½ × 14⅜″*

50. Call It Madness. *1958. Collage. 11½ × 14⅜″*

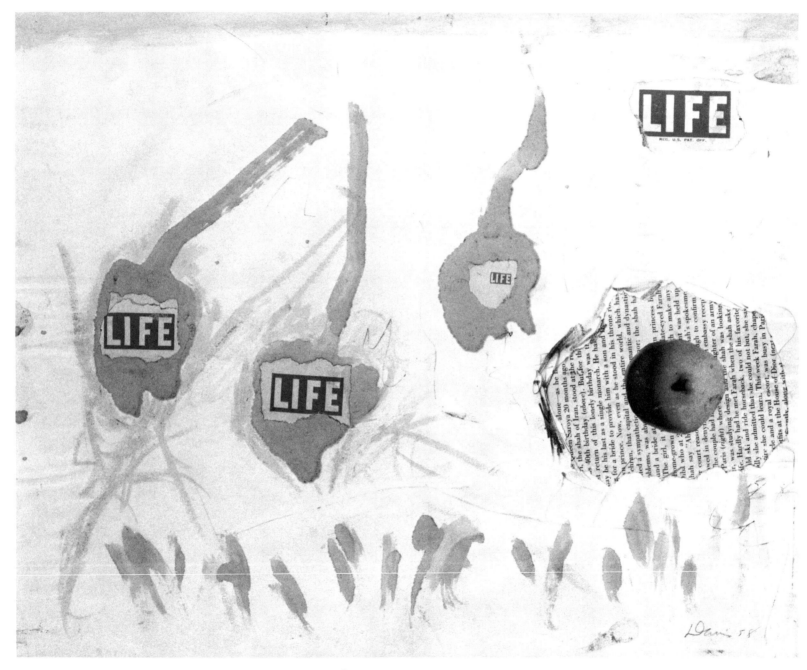

51. *Life. 1958. Collage. 11¼ × 14⅝″*

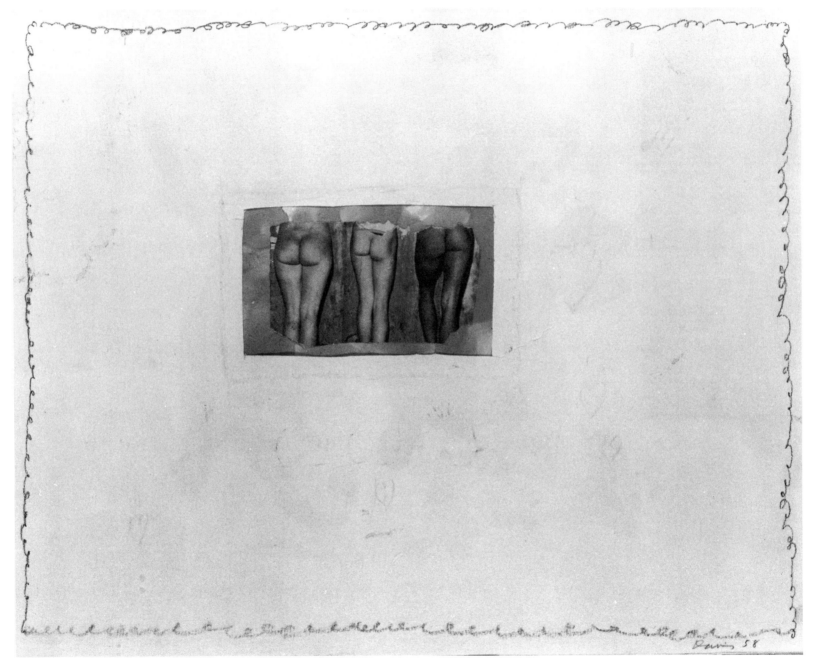

52. *Rear View. 1958. Collage. 11¼ × 14⅝".*
The Solomon R. Guggenheim Museum, New York

53

53. Salt of the Earth. *1958. Collage. 10¼ × 14⅜"*

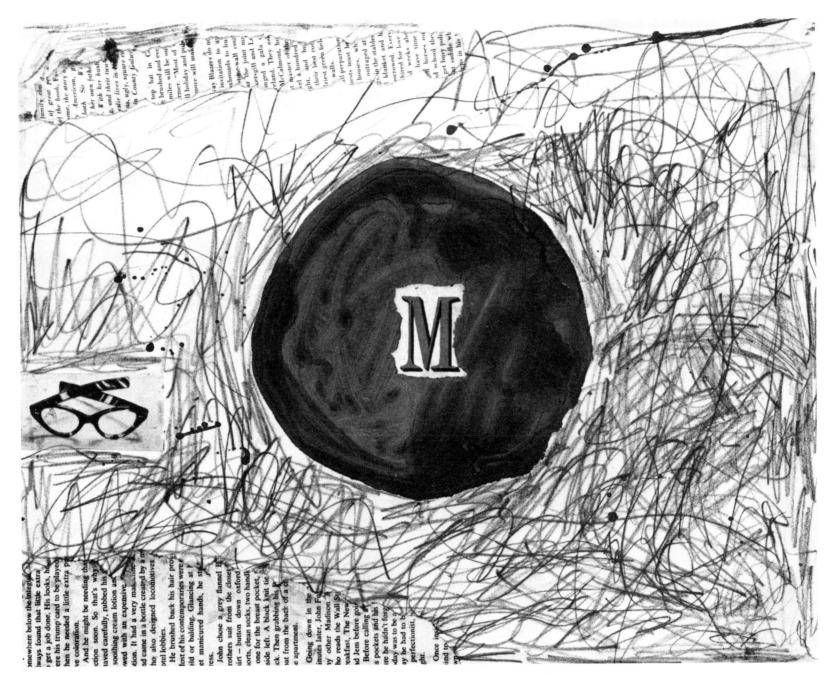

54. Eye Glasses. 1958. Collage. 11¼ × 14½"

55. *Lavoris. 1958. Collage with pencil and crayon.* 11¼ × 14½"

56. *$4.95. 1958. Collage with pencil.* 11½ × 14½"

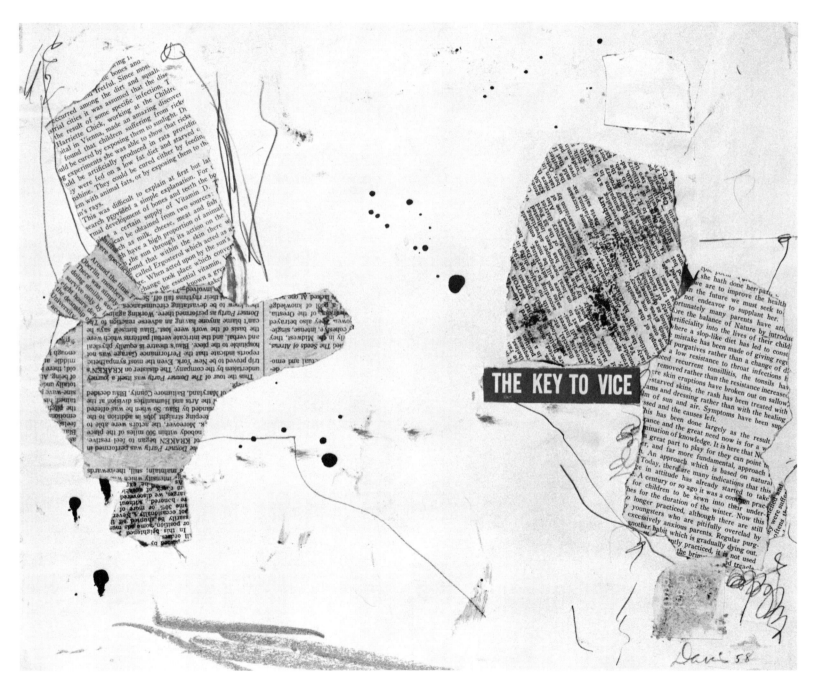

THE KEY TO VICE

57. Key to Vice. *1958. Collage. 11½ × 14½"*

58. Girl and Stripes. *1958. Collage. 11½ × 14⅜"*

59. Reclining Lady. 1958. Collage. 11½ × 14⅜"

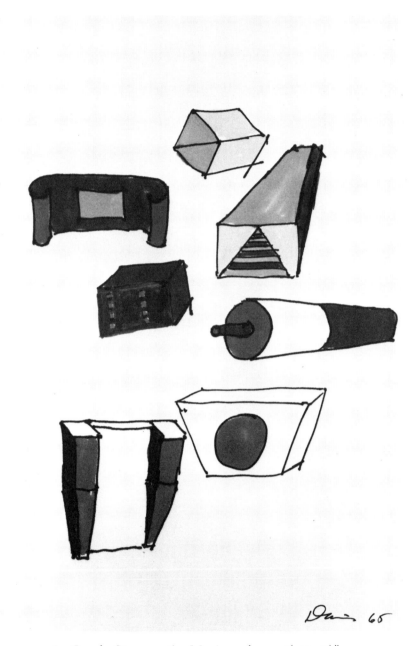

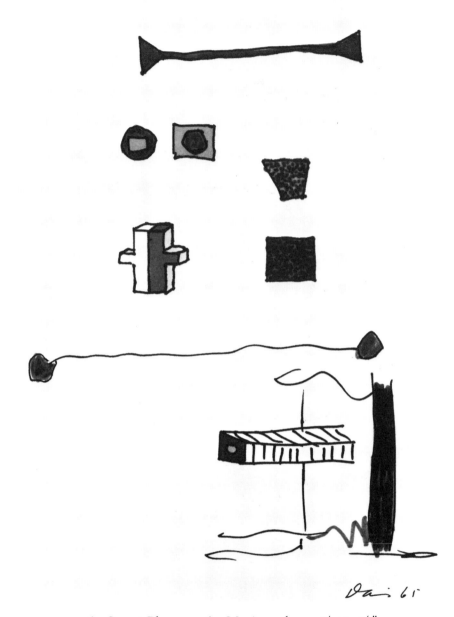

60. Candy Store. *1965. Magic marker. 10¾ × 7¾"*

61. Secret Places. *1965. Magic marker. 10¾ × 7¾"*

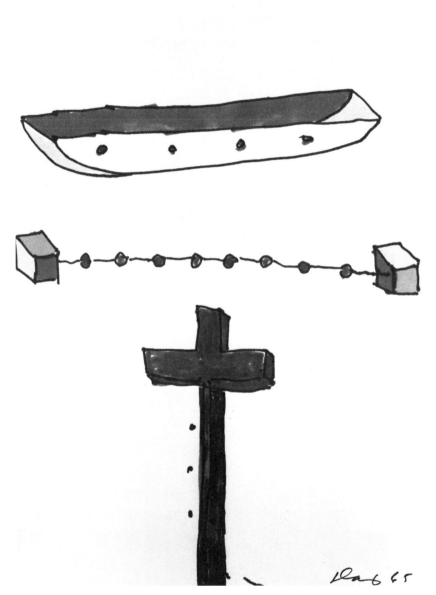

62. Boat and Cross. *1965. Magic marker.* $10^3/_4 \times 7^3/_4$"

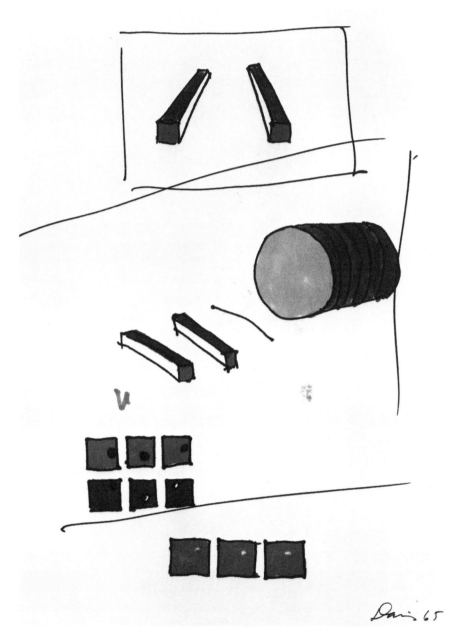

63. Jack in the Box. *1965. Magic marker.* $10^3/_4 \times 7^3/_4$"

64. Five Bird Houses. *1974. Pencil and crayon. 14 × 16½″*

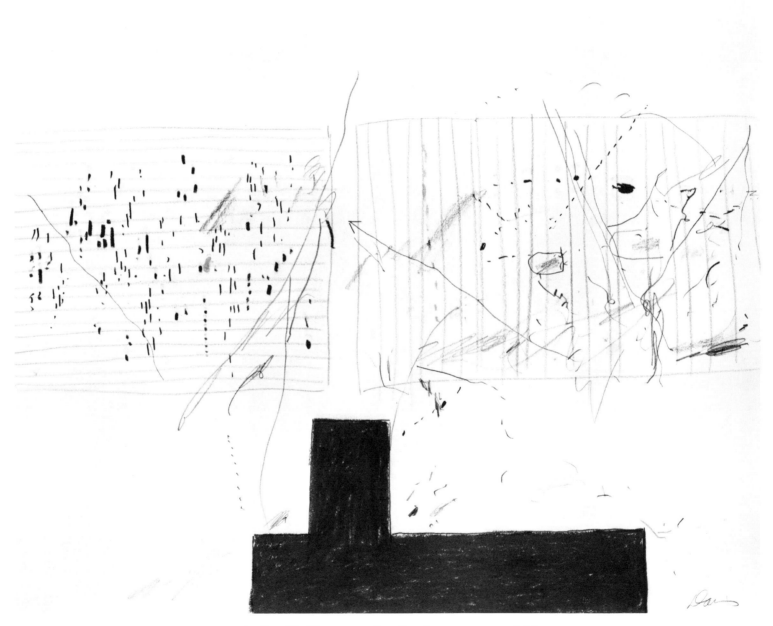

65. Devil's Hut. *1974. Pencil and crayon. 14 × 16½"*

66. Brain Waves. 1974. Pencil and crayon. 14 × 16½"

67. Clean Sweep. 1974. Pencil and crayon. 14 × 16½″

68. Side Kick. *1974. Pencil and crayon. 14 × 16 ½"*

69. Sidewalk Superintendent. *1974. Pencil and crayon. 14 × 16½″*

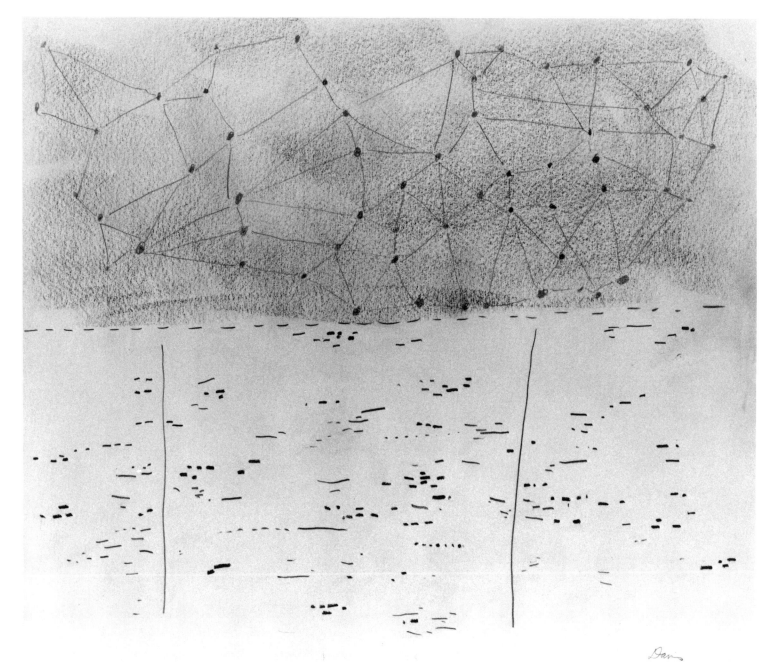

70. Secret Signs. 1976. Pencil and crayon. 14 × 16½″

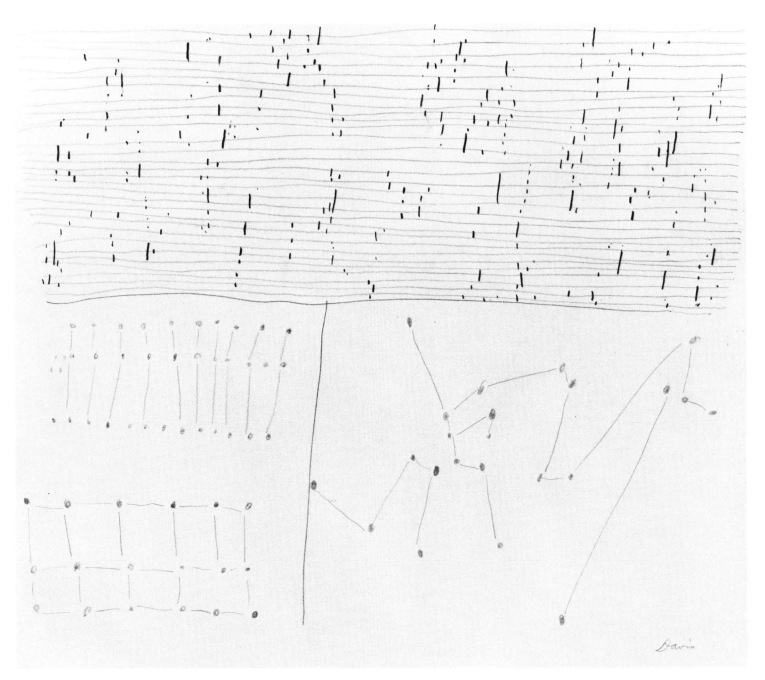

71. Celestial Score. *1976. Pencil and crayon. 14 × 16½"*

72. High Pockets. *1976. Pastel and pencil. 14 × 16¾″*

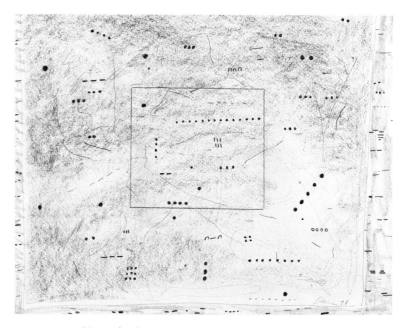

74. City Block. *1976. Pastel and pencil. 14 × 16¾″*

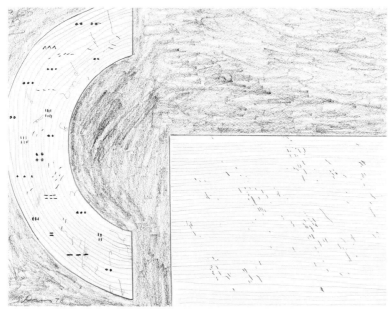

73. Dots and Dashes. *1976. Pencil. 14 × 16¾″*

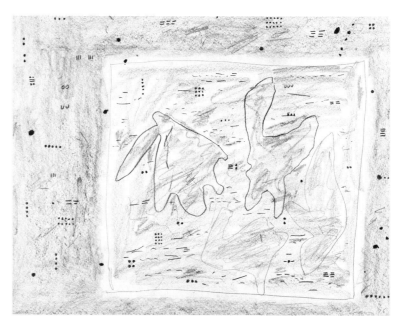

75. Eskimo Map. *1976. Pastel and pencil. 14 × 16¾″*

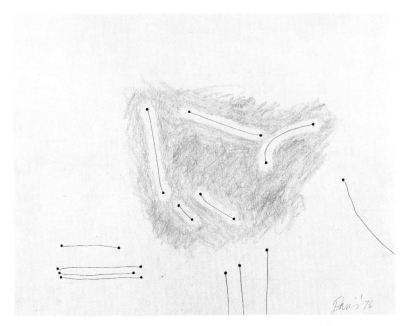

76. Mendel's Law. *1976. Pencil. 14 × 16¾″*

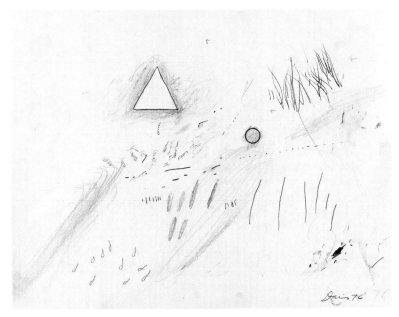

77. Triangle and Circle. *1976. Pencil. 14 × 16¾″*

78. Fool's Garden. *1976. Pencil and crayon. 14 × 16¾"*

79. Shanty. 1976. Pencil. 14 × 17"

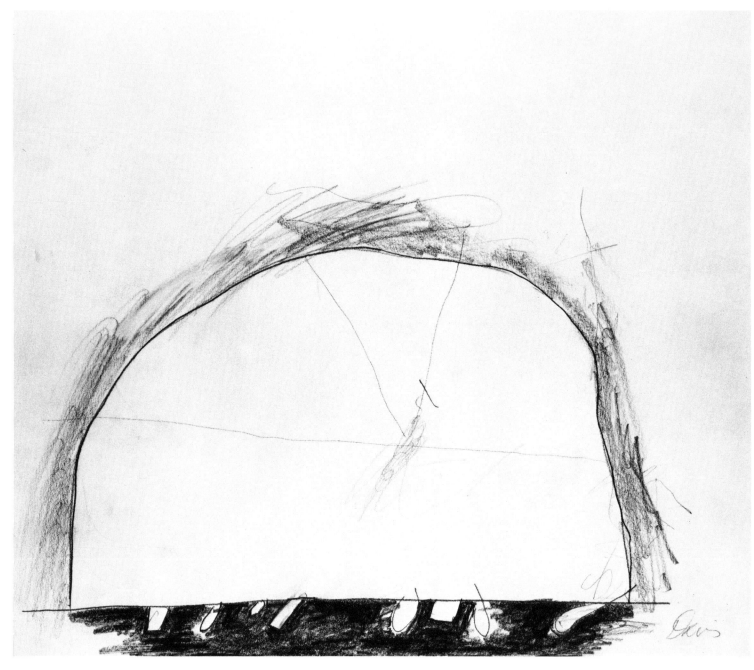

80. Magic Turtle. *1976. Pencil. 14 × 16¾"*

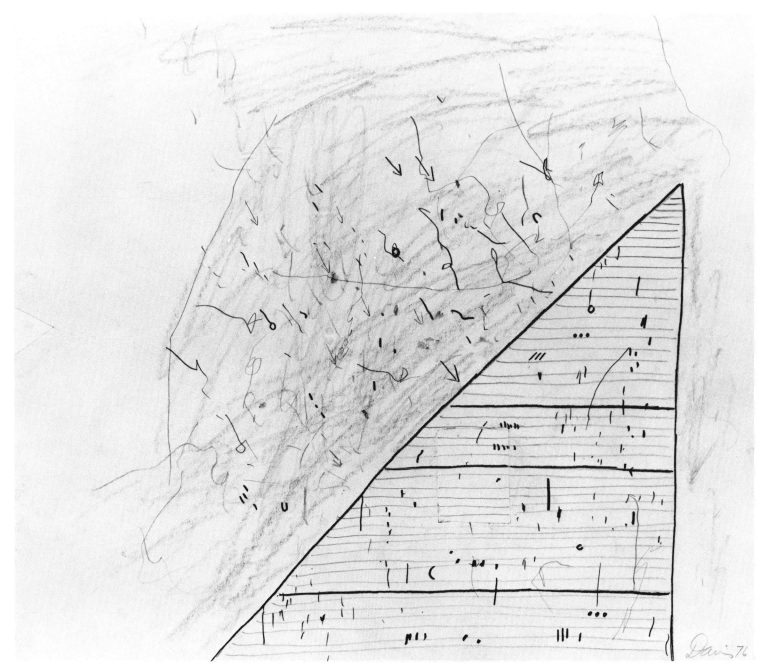

81. Einstein Pyramid. *1976. Pencil and crayon. 14 × 16½"*

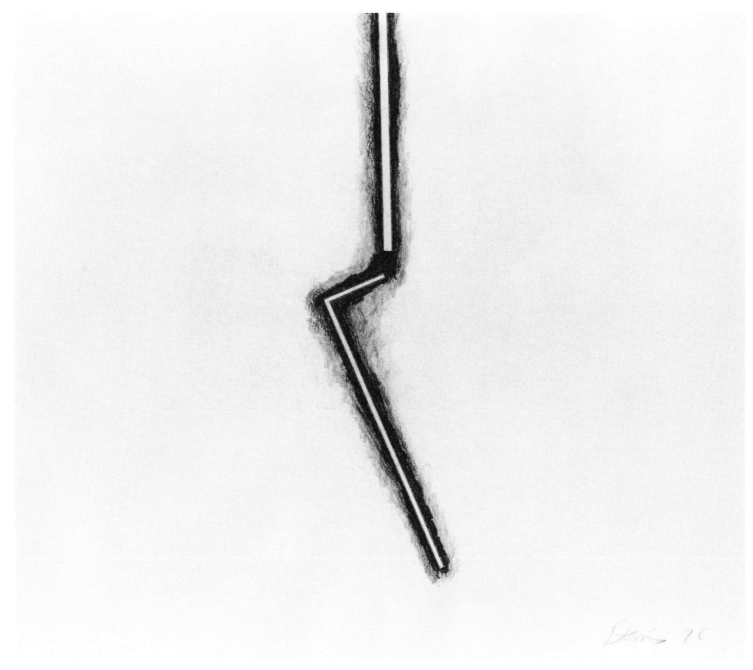

82. Broken Stripe. *1976. Pencil. 14 × 16½".*
Collection Andrew Crispo, New York

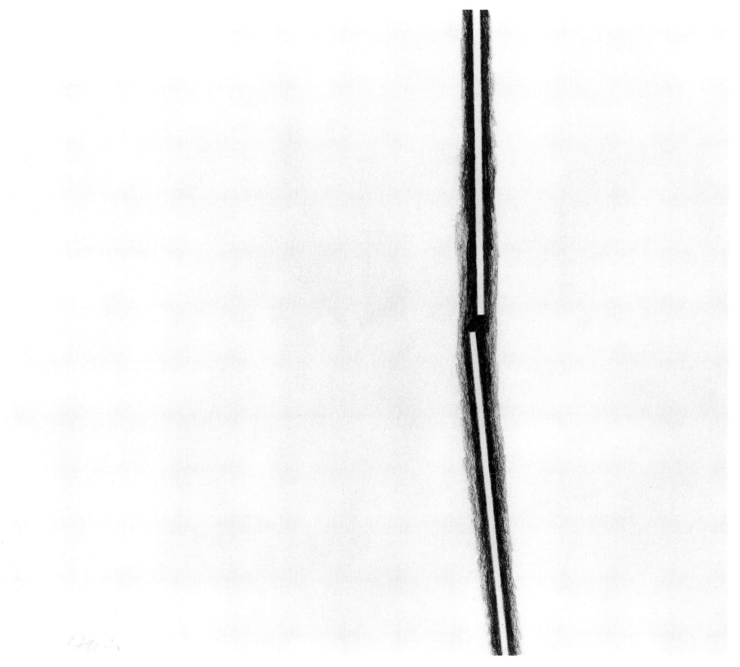

83. Broken Stripe. *1976. Pencil. 14 × 16½".*
Collection Andrew Crispo, New York

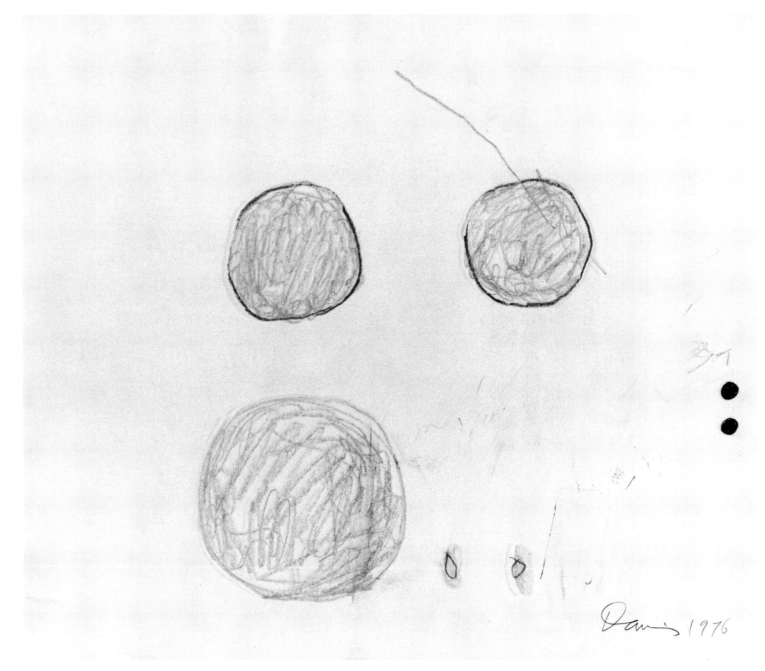

84. Three Circles. *1976. Pencil and crayon. 14 × 16⅝″*

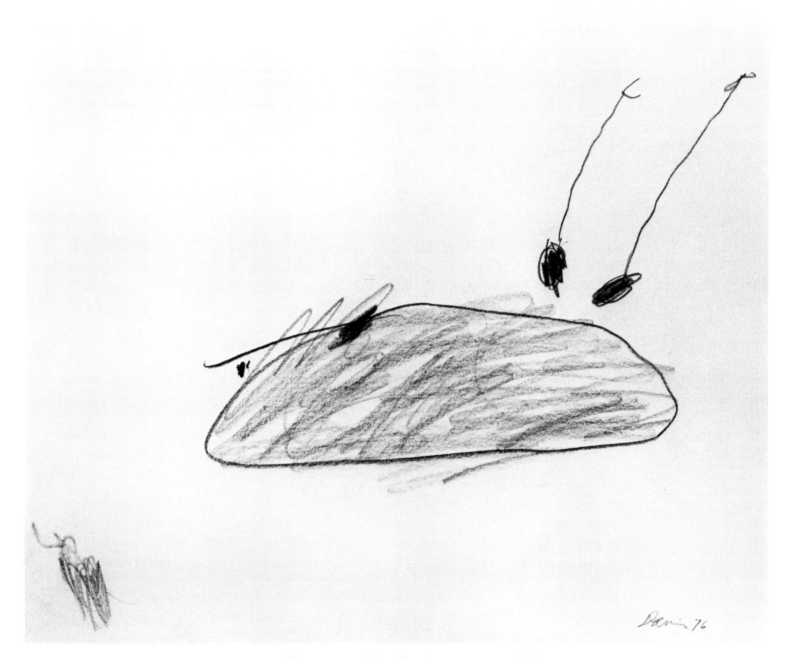

85. Playpen. *1976. Pencil and crayon. 14 × 16½"*

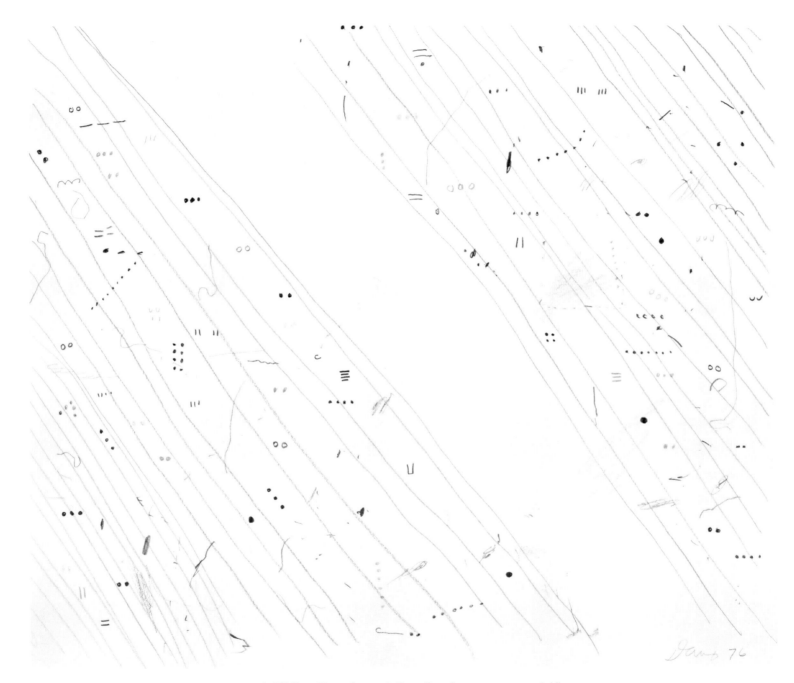

86. Sliding Board. *1976. Pencil and crayon. 14 × 16¾″*

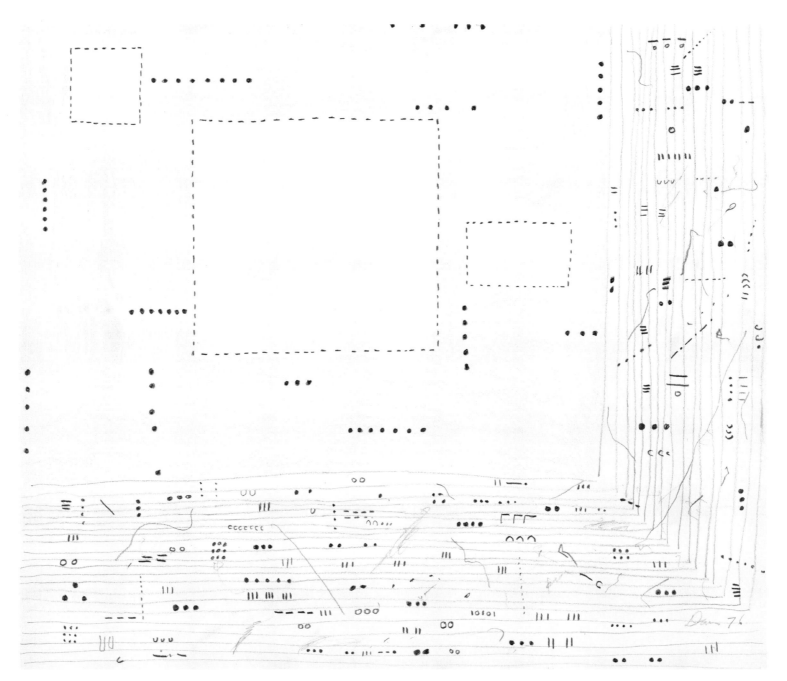

87. Peter's Puzzle. *Pencil and crayon. 14 × 16¾″*

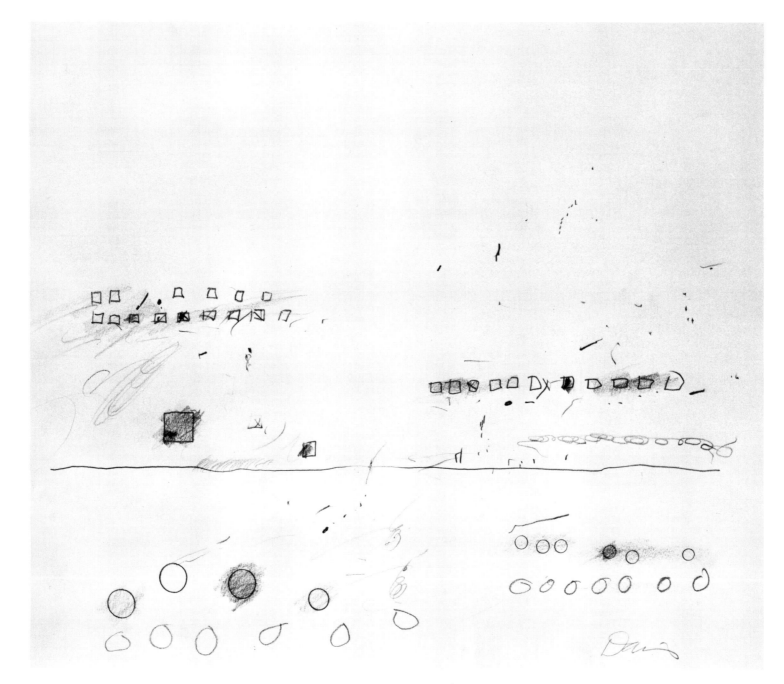

88. Keeping Score. *1976. Pencil. 14 × 16½″*

89. Funny Bones. *1976. Pencil. 14 × 16½"*

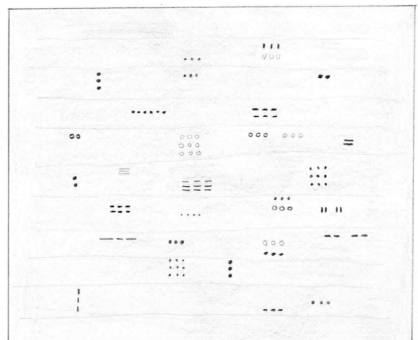

90. Mystery Guest. *1976. Pencil on paper. 14 × 16¾"*

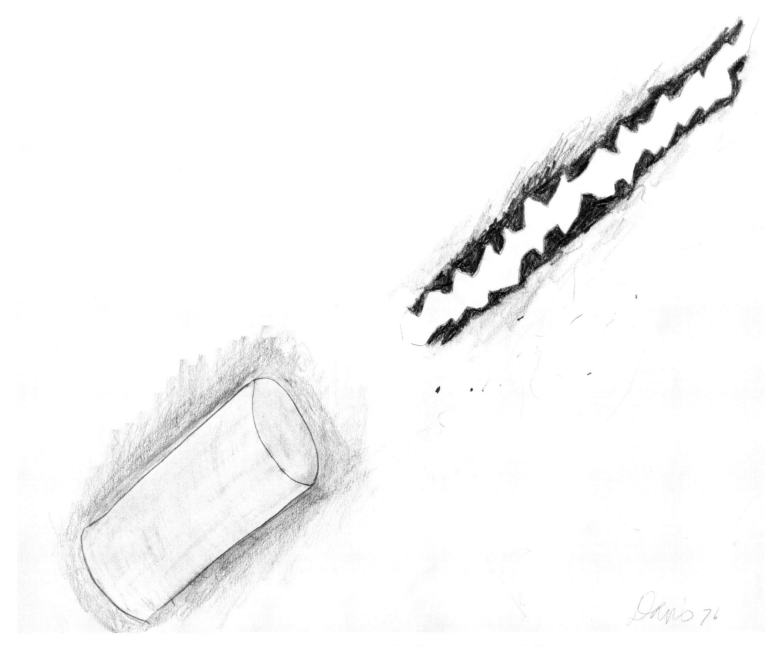

85

91. Noon Meeting. 1976. Pencil on paper. 14 × 16¾″

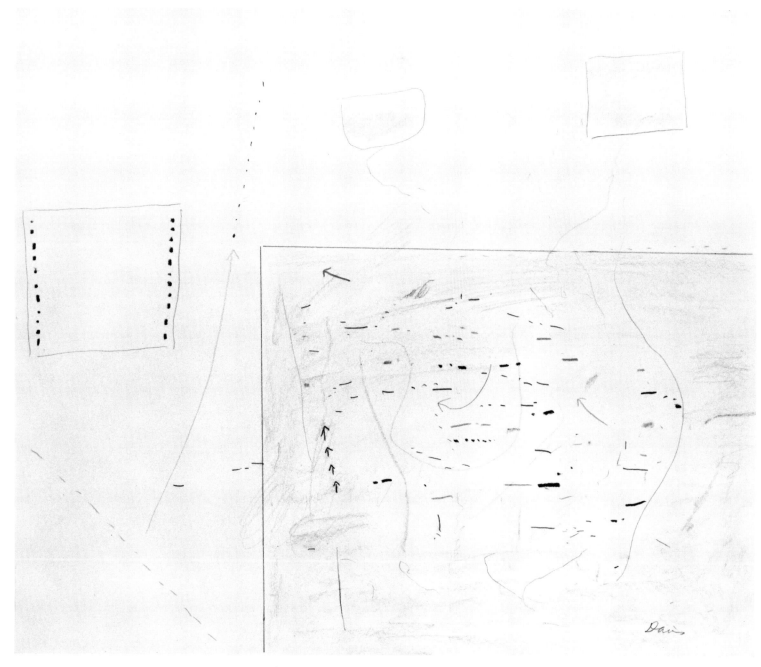

92. Klee's Way. *1976. Pencil and crayon. 14 × 16¾"*

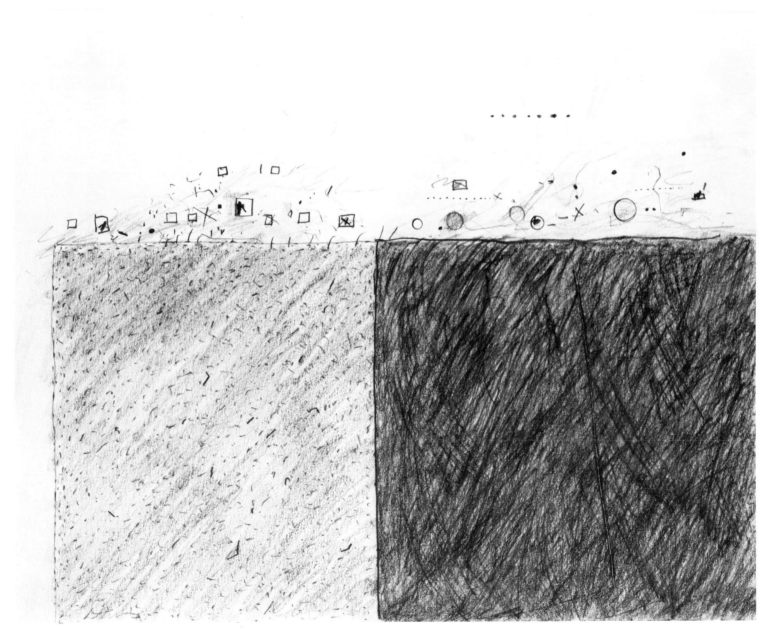

93. Myopic Fence. *1976. Pencil. 14 × 16½"*

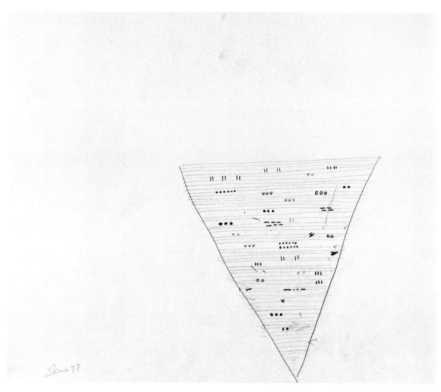

94. Inverted Triangle. *1977. Pencil and crayon. 14 × 16¾"*

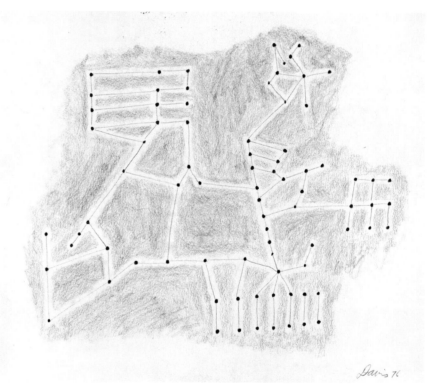

95. Game Plan. *1976. Pencil. 14 × 16¾"*

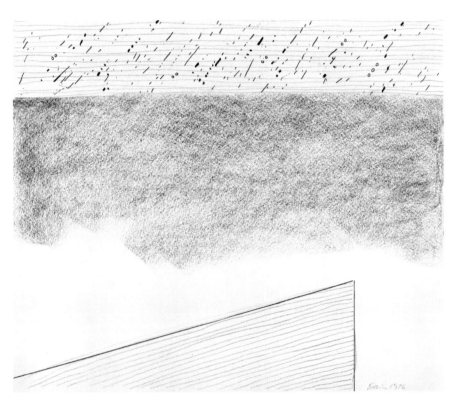

96. Euclidian Landscape. *1975. Pencil. 14 × 16¾"*

97. Toy Drawer. *1976. Pencil. 14 × 16¾"*

98. Hobby Horse. *1976. Pencil and crayon. 14 × 16¾"*

99. Fallout. *1977. Pencil and crayon. 14 × 16¾"*

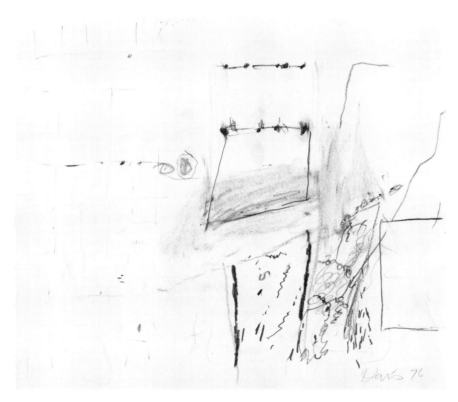

100. Lunar Feast. *1976. Pencil and crayon. 14 × 16¾"*

101. Crazy Horse. *1978. Pencil and crayon. 14 × 16¾"*

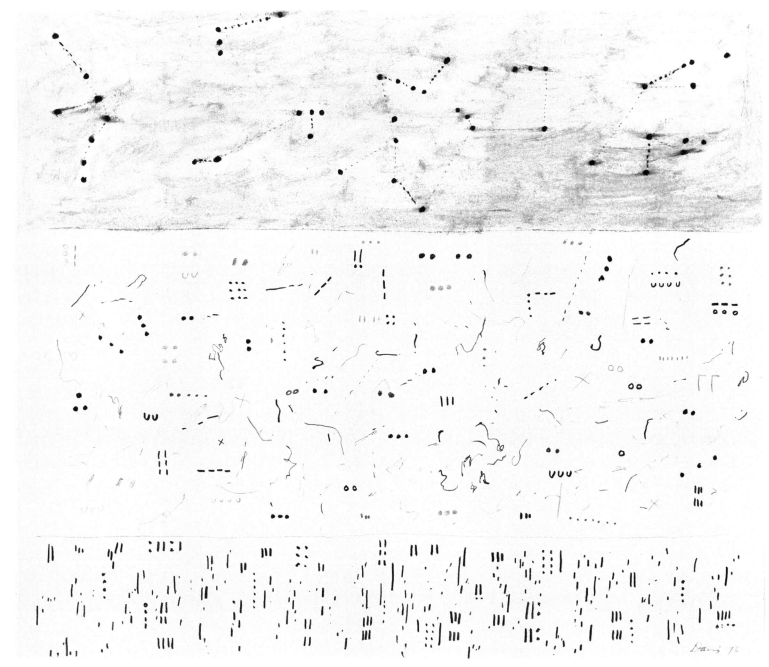

102. Deep Six. *1976. Pencil and crayon. 13¾ × 16⅝"*

93

103. Papal Jamboree. *1978. Pencil and crayon. 13¾ × 16⅝"*

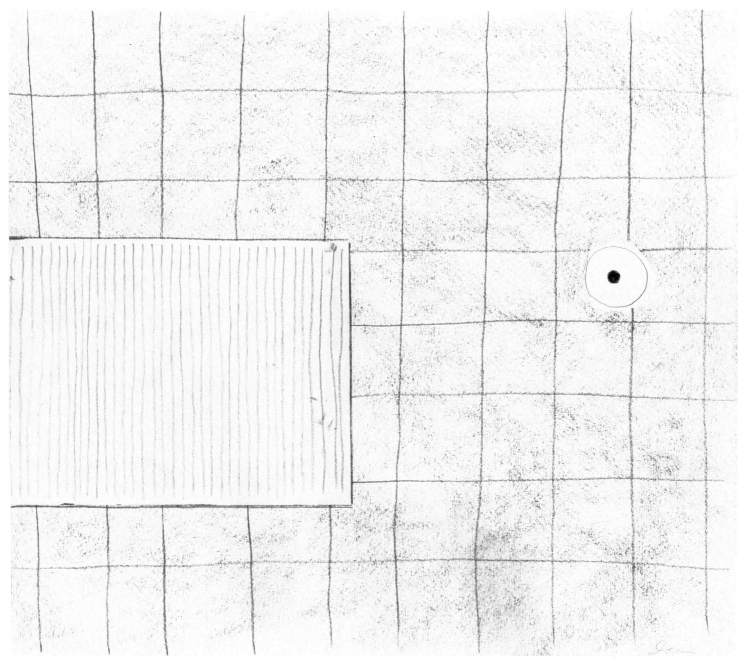

104. Ball and Cage. *1978. Pencil. 14 × 16¾″*

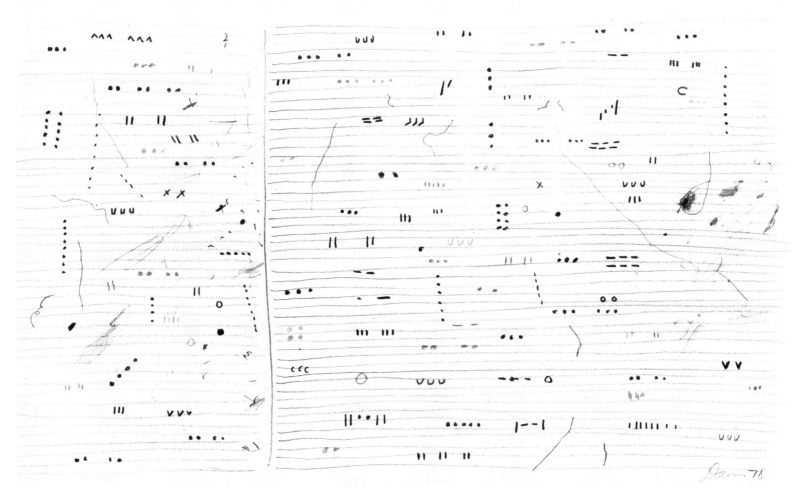

105. Song Bird. 1978. Pencil and crayon. 13⅜ × 16⅞″

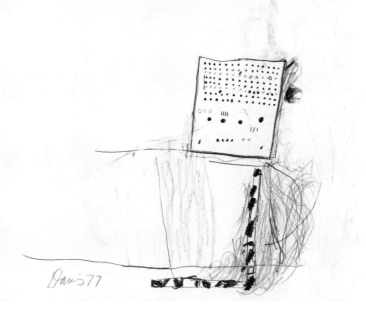

106. Two Balls. *1978. Pencil and crayon. 14 × 16¾"*

107. Third Avenue. *1977. Pencil and crayon. 14 × 16¾"*

108. Nocturnal Alphabet. *1977. Pencil and crayon. 14 × 16¾"*

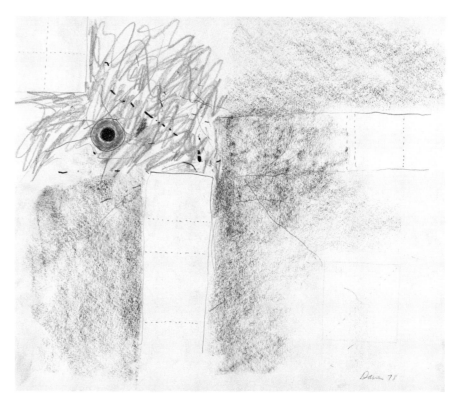

109. Halley's Comet. *1978. Pencil and crayon. 14 × 16¾"*

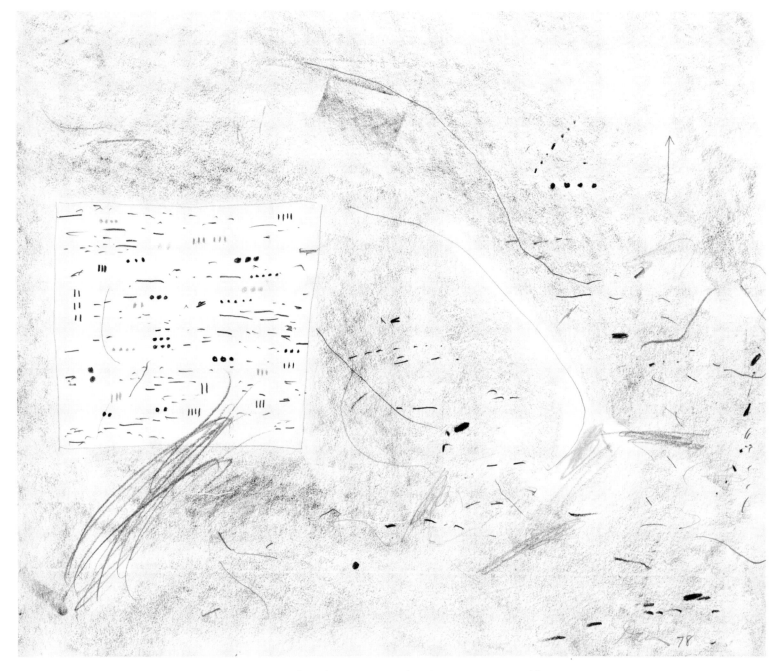

110. North Pole. *1978. Pencil and crayon. 14 × 16¾"*

111. Mardi Gras. *1978. Pencil and crayon. 14 × 16½"*

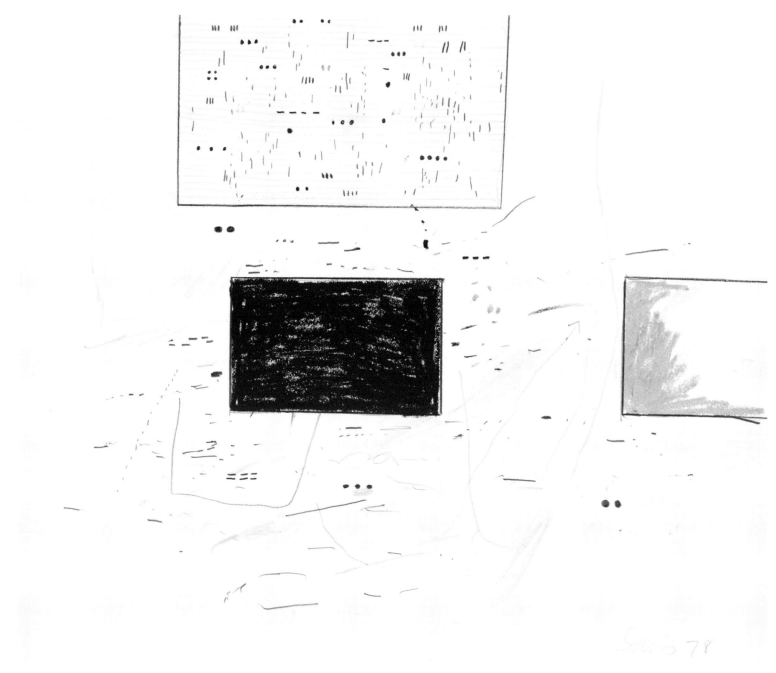

112. Treasure Chest. *1978. Pencil and crayon. 14 × 16¾″*

113. Sky Ruler. *1978. Pencil and crayon. 14 × 16¾"*

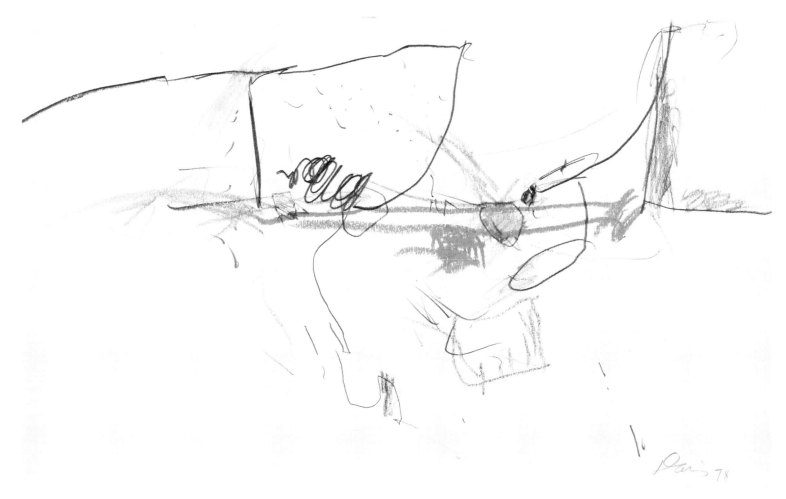

114. Jumping Jack. *1978. Pencil and crayon. 14 × 16¾"*

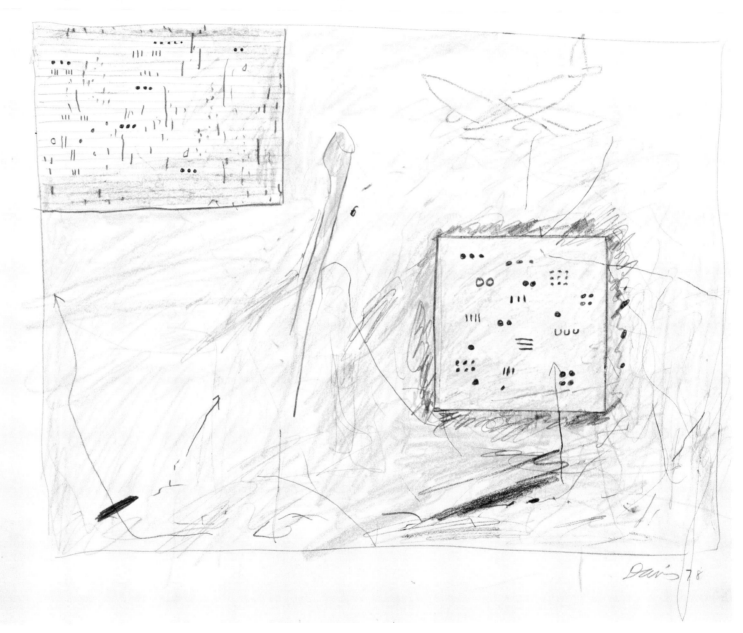

115. Directions. *1978. Pencil and crayon. 14 × 16¾"*

116. Coffin Corner. 1978. Pencil and crayon. 14 × 16¾"

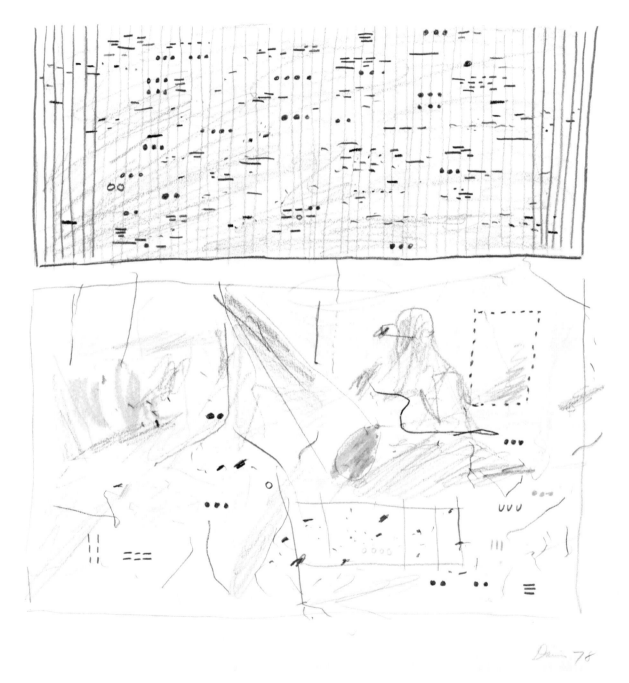

117. Back Yard. 1978. Pencil and crayon. 14 × 16¾″

118. Cross Walk. *1977. Ink. 15 × 20"*

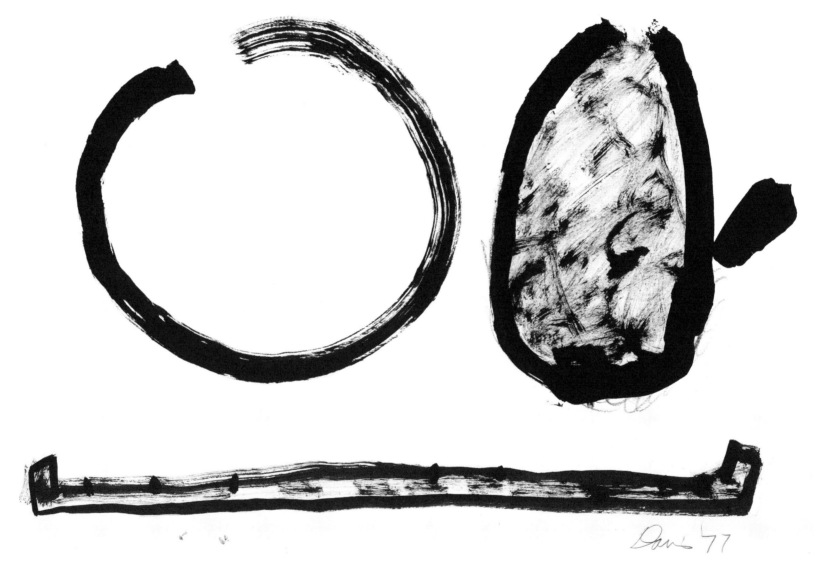

119. Indian Signs. *1977. Ink. 15 × 20"*

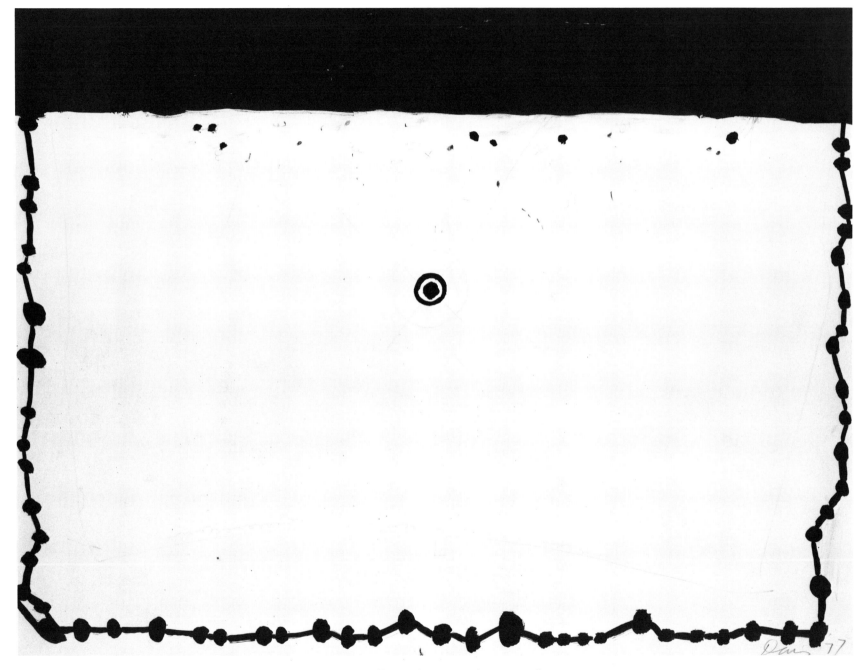

120. Bull's Eye. *1977. Ink. 15 × 20"*

121. Iron Flower. *1977. Ink. 15 × 20″*

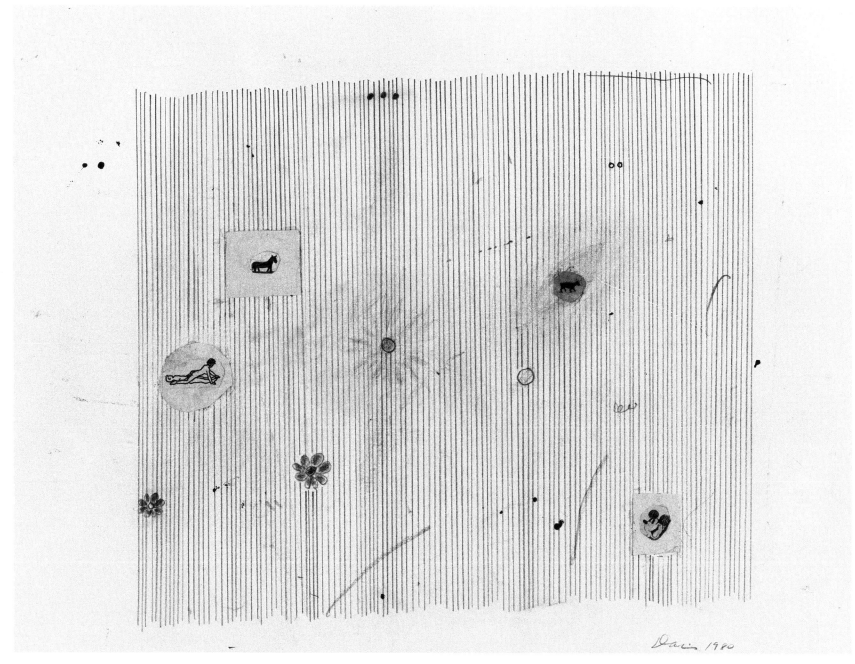

122. Central Park. *1980. Collage with pencil and crayon. 14⅞ × 19⅞″*

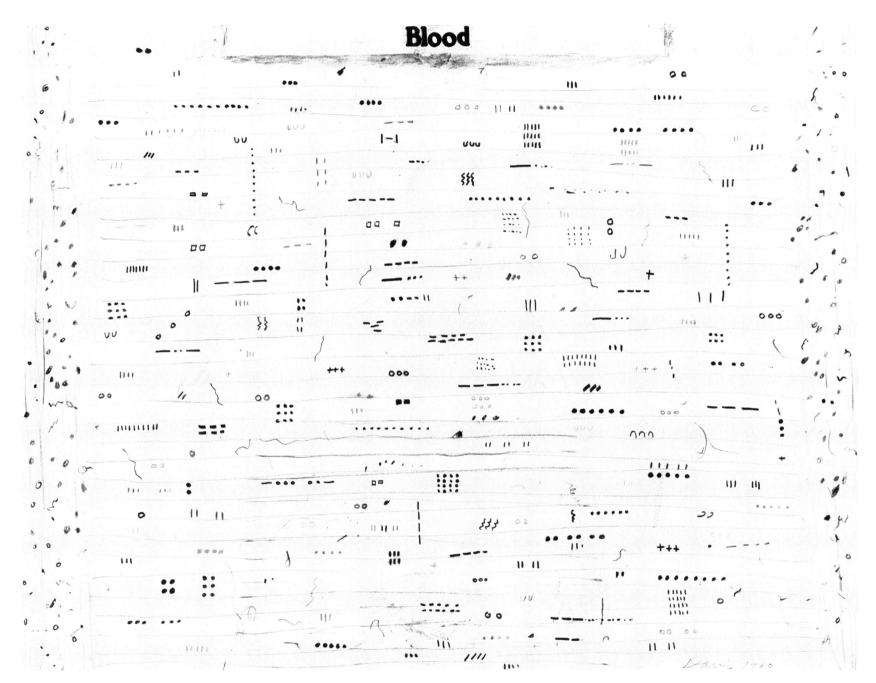

123. Blood. *1980. Collage with pencil and crayon. 14⅞ × 19⅞"*

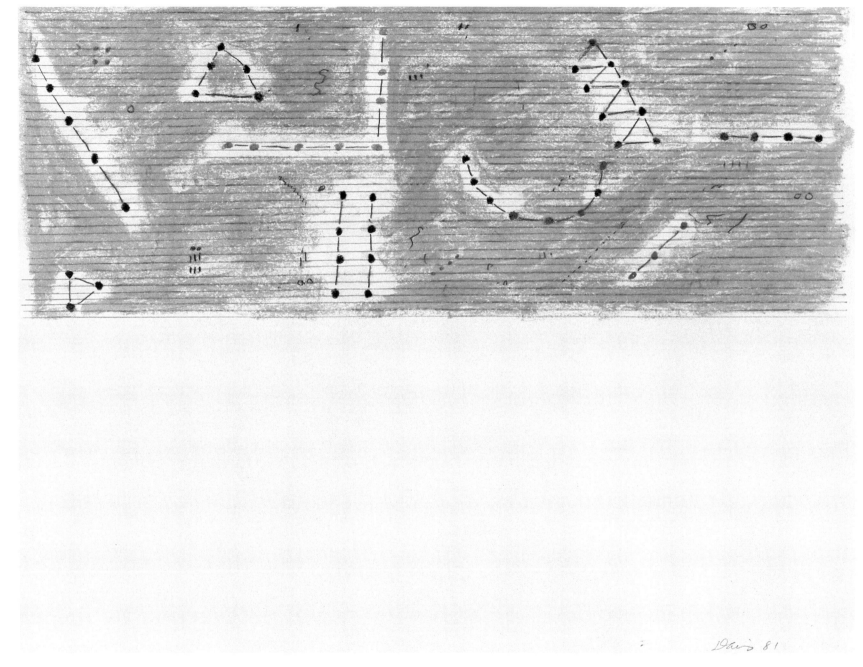

124. Constellation. *1981. Pencil and crayon. 15 × 20"*

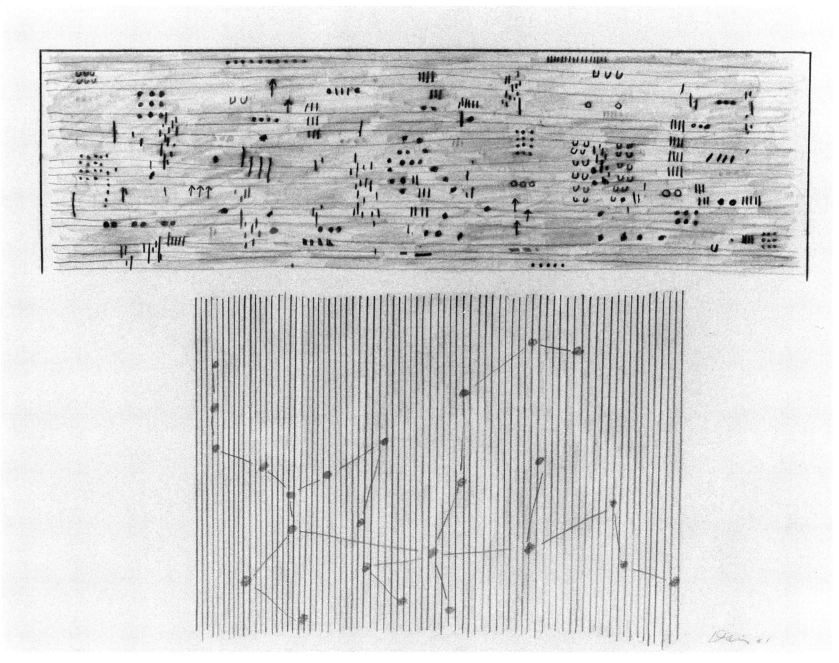

125. Islam. 1981. Pencil and crayon. 14⅞ × 19⅞"

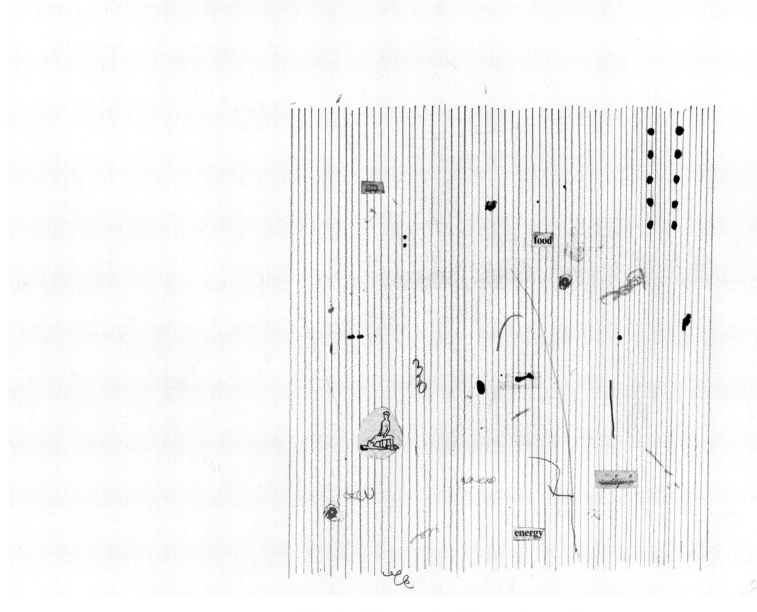

126. Food and Energy. *1981. Collage. 14¾ × 19¾"*

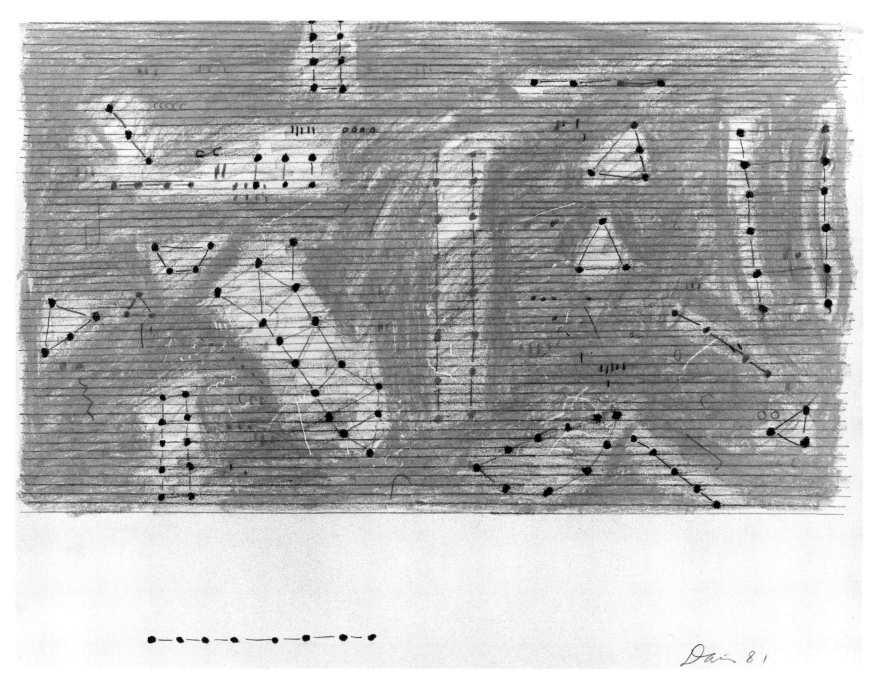

127. Sky Code. 1981. Pastel, pencil, and crayon. 14¾ × 19⅞"

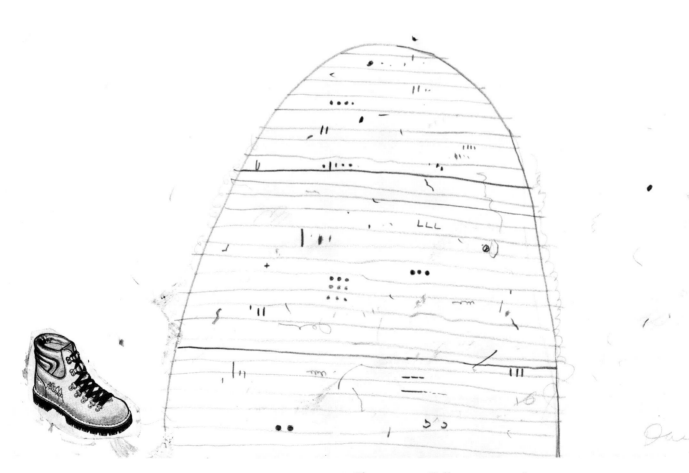

128. Shoe. *1980. Collage. 15 × 20"*

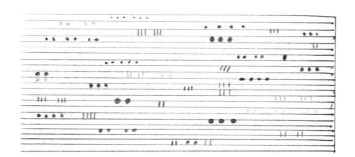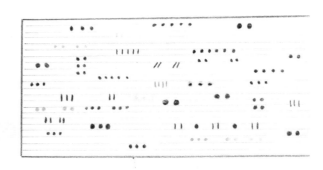

129. Chicken. *1980. Collage. 15 × 20″*

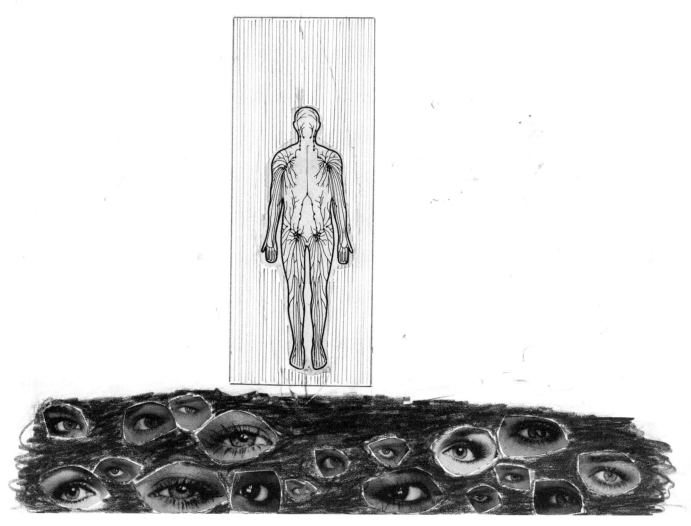

130. Watching. *1980*. Collage. *15 × 20"*

131. Black Cat. 1980. Collage. 15 × 20"

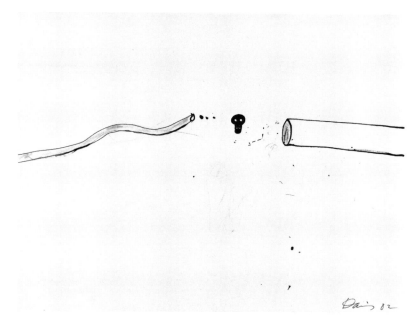

132. Eternal Riddle. *1982. Ink and crayon. 15 × 20"*

134. Noon Flame. *1982. Ink and crayon. 15 × 20"*

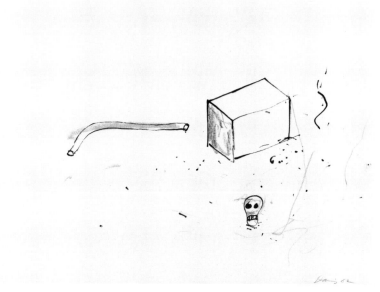

133. Box and Tube. *1982. Ink and crayon. 15 × 20"*

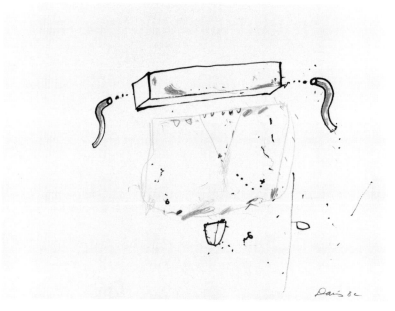

135. Pocket Book. *1982. Ink and crayon. 15 × 20"*

136. Traffic. 1981. Ink. 15 × 18"

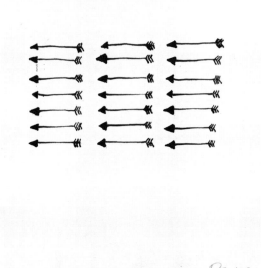

137. 21 Arrows. 1981. Ink. 15 × 20"

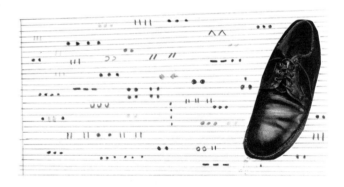

138. Two Shoes. *1980. Collage. 15 × 20"*

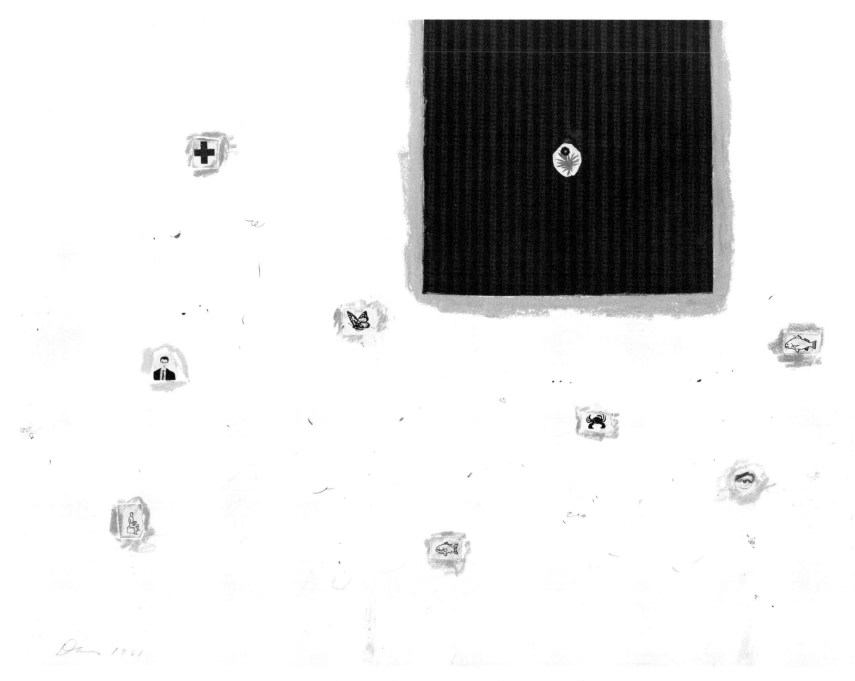

139. Flower and Stripes. *1981. Collage. 15 × 20″*

140. Family Car. *1981. Collage. 11 × 17″*

141. Pride and Joy. *1981. Collage. 11 × 17″*

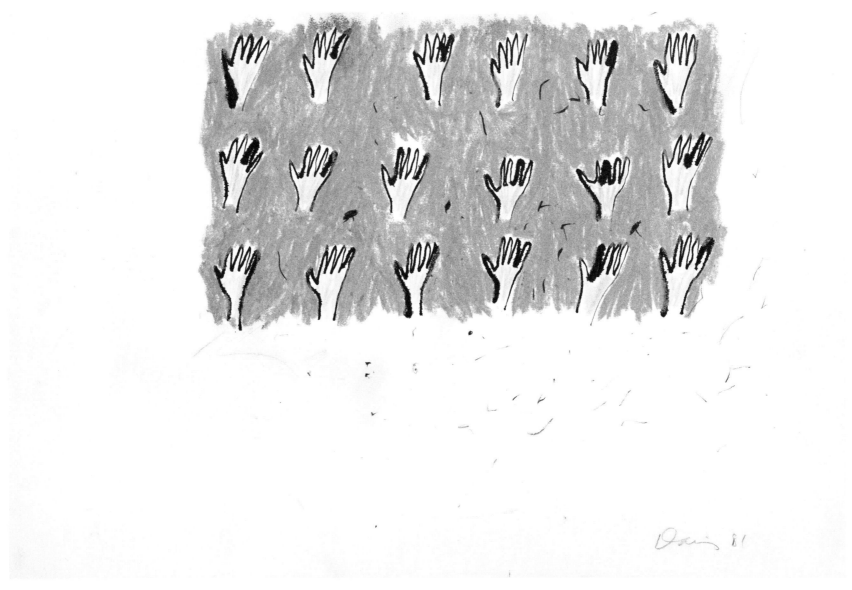

142. Hands. *1980. Ink and pastel. 13 × 20″*

143. Spectacles. *1981. Ink. 11 × 17″*

144. Three Men. *1981. Collage. 13¾ × 19¾"*

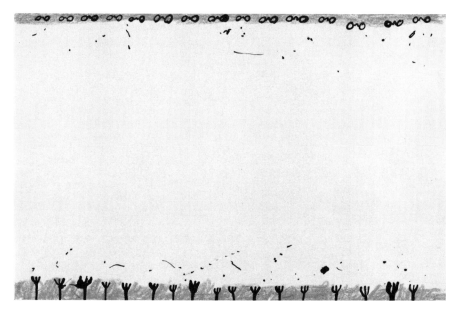

145. Forks and Glasses. *1981. Ink and crayon. 11 × 17″*

147. Cars. *1981. Ink and crayon. 11 × 17″*

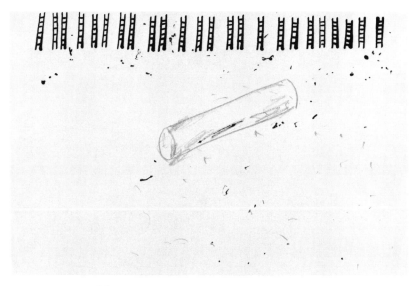

146. Ladders and Tube. *1981. Ink and crayon. 11 × 17″*

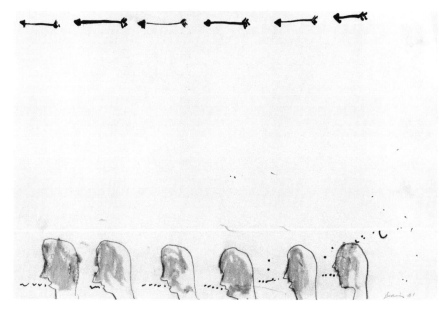

148. Arrows and Heads. *1981. Ink and crayon. 11 × 17″*

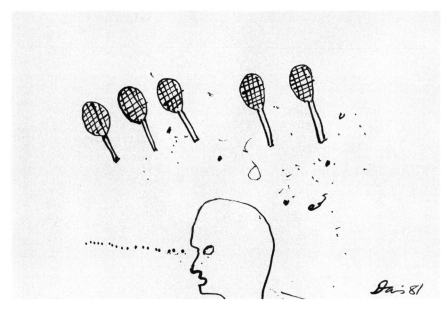

149. Dreams. *1981. Ink. 11 × 17"*

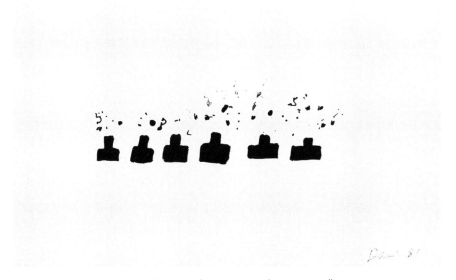

150. Fireworks. *1981. Ink. 11 × 17"*

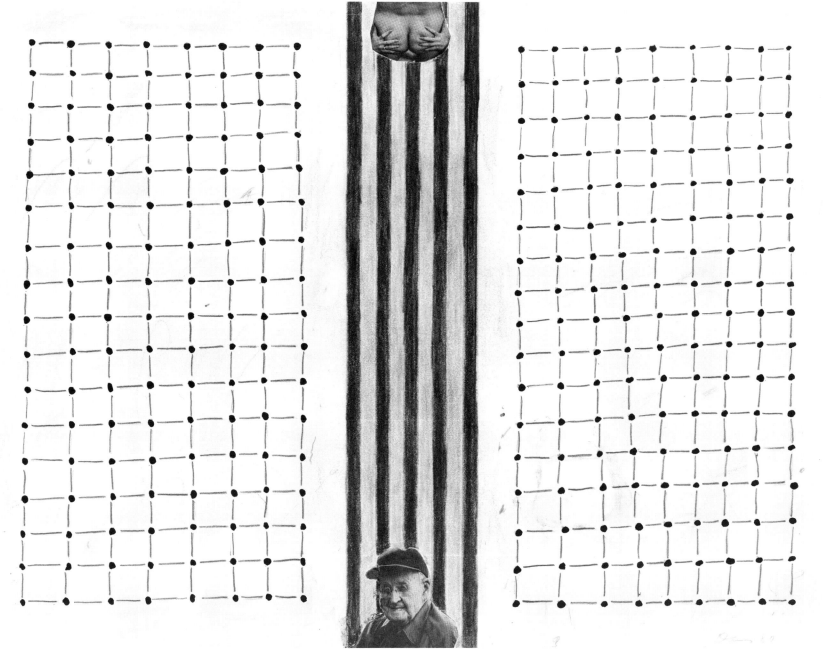

151. The Good Life. *1980. Collage. 15 × 20″*

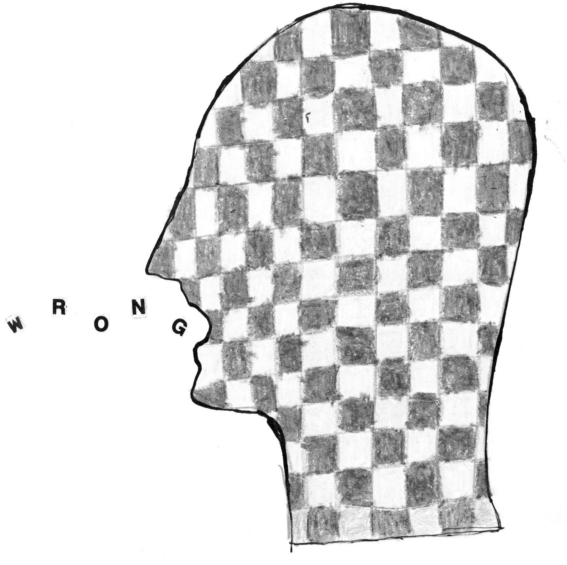

W R O N G

152. *Wrong. 1981. Collage. 15 × 20"*

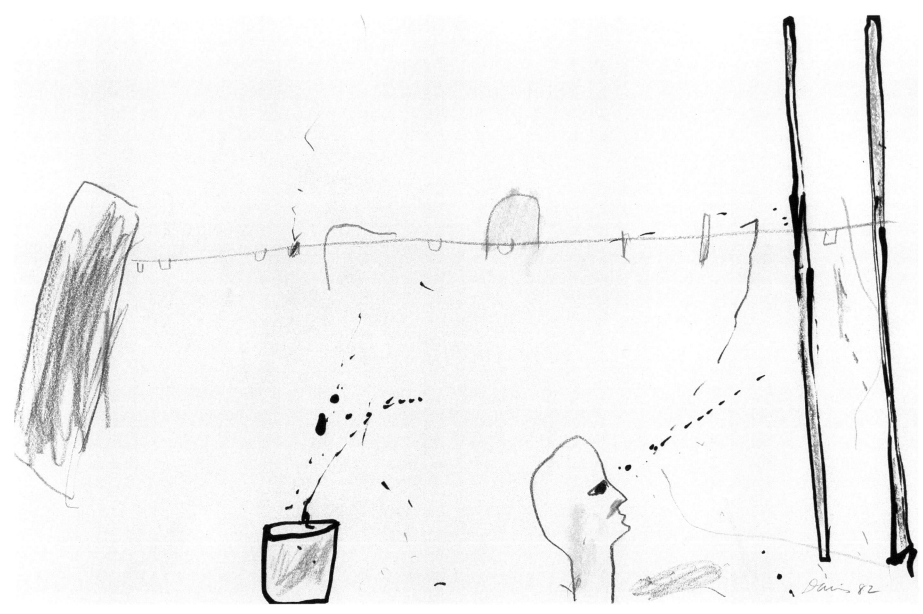

153. Clothes Line. *1982. Ink and crayon.* 10¾ × 17″

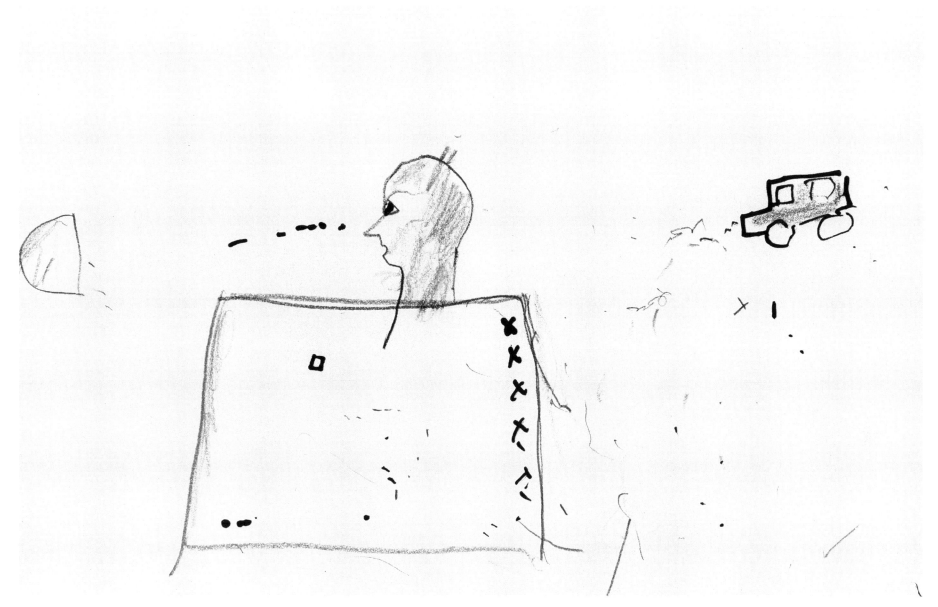

154. Car Chase. *1982. Ink and crayon. 10¾ × 17″*

155. *Spy. 1982. Ink and crayon. 11 × 17"*

156. Heavenly Grid. *1982. Ink and crayon. 11 × 17″*

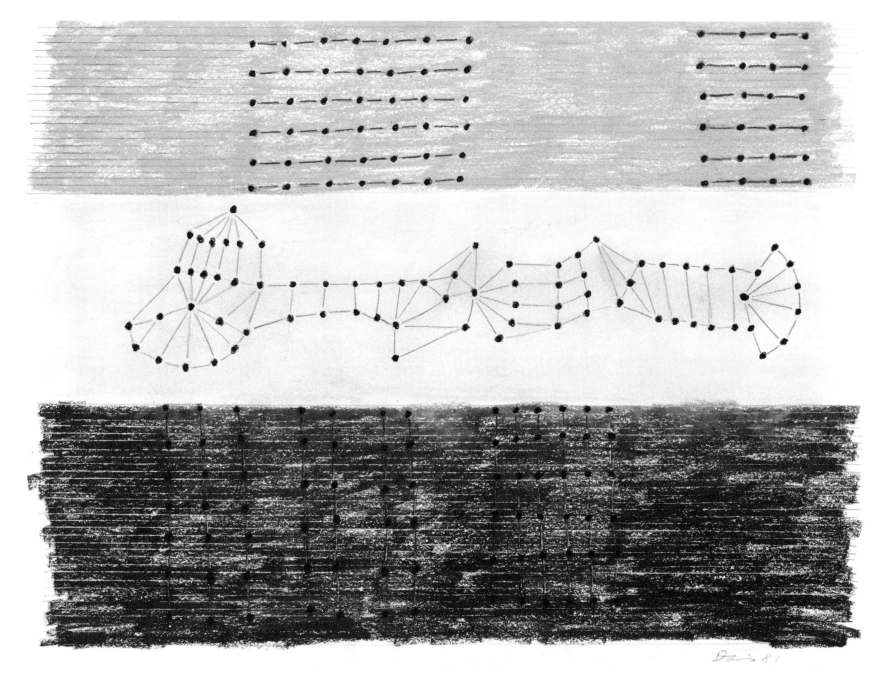

157. Sky Puzzle. *1981. Pencil and pastel. 15 × 20"*

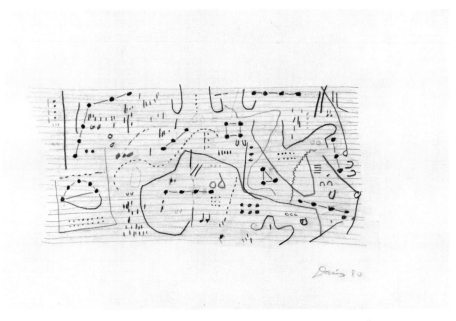

158. Sweet Talk. 1980. Pencil and crayon. 11 × 17″

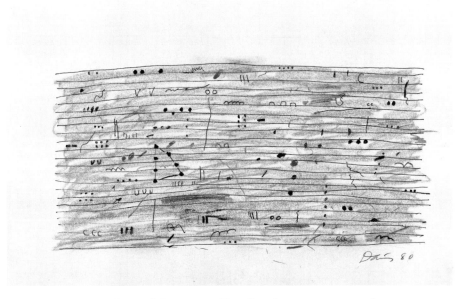

159. Space Man. 1980. Pencil and crayon. 11 × 17″

160. Scatter Brain. *1981. Ink. 14⅞ × 19⅞"*

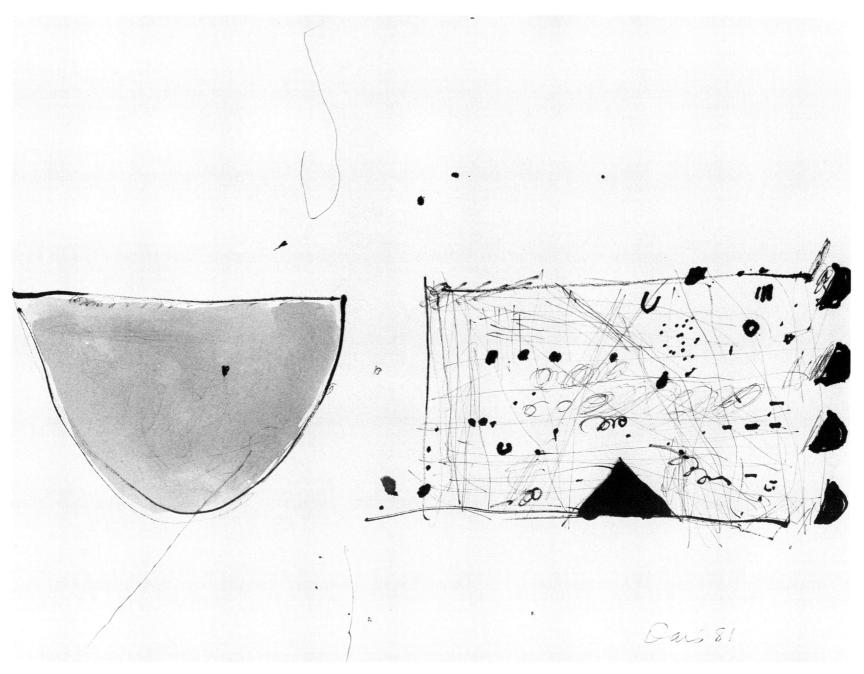

161. Socrates' Cup. *1981. Ink. 14⅞ × 19⅞″*

162. Right Angles. *1981. Ink and wash.* 14⅞ × 19⅞"

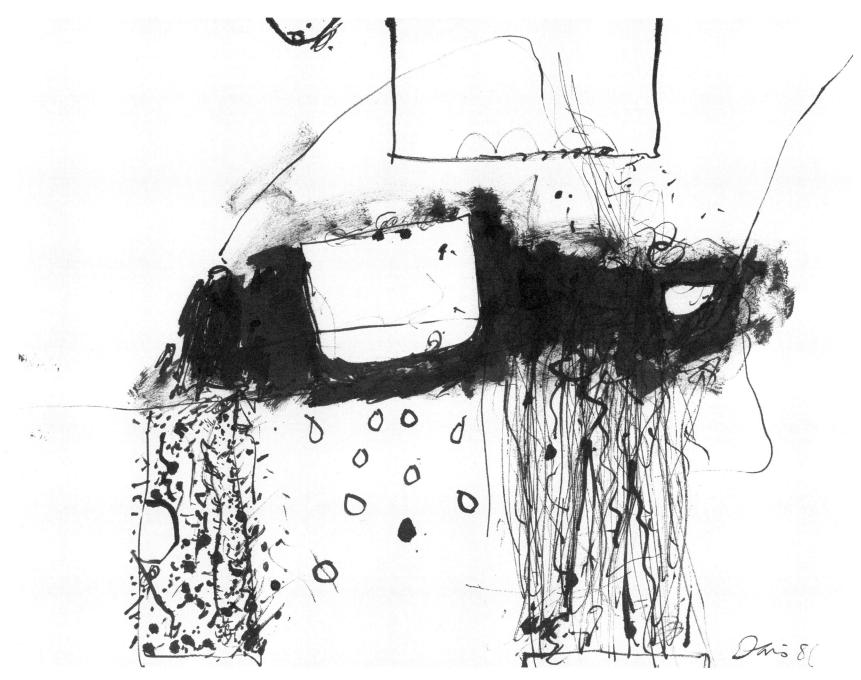

163. Box Car. *1981. Ink. 14⅞ × 20″*

164. Tornado. 1981. Ink. 14⅞ × 20″

165. Wild Cat. *1981. Ink and wash. 14¾ × 20″*

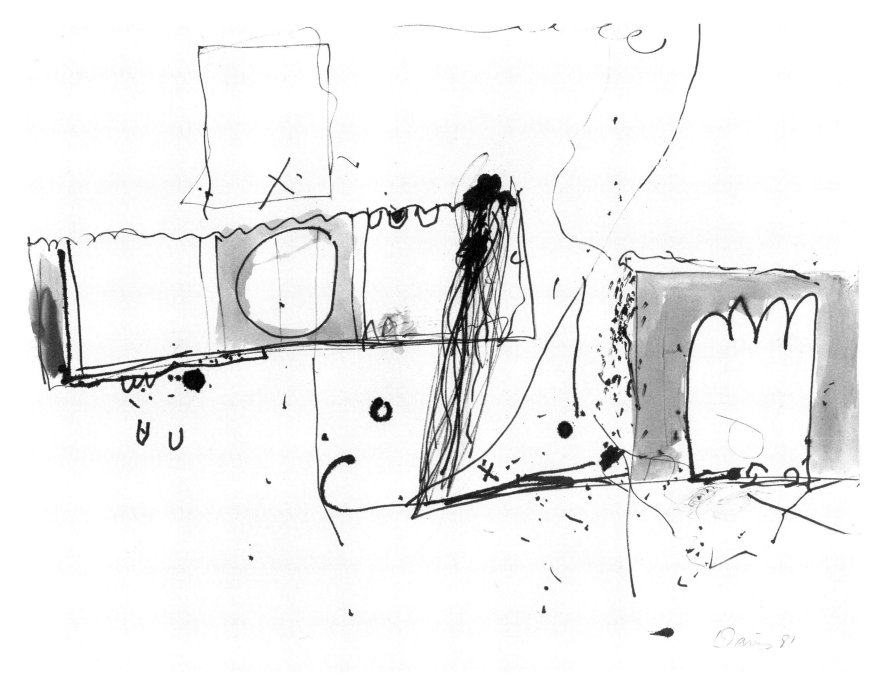

166. Cross Fire. *1981. Ink and wash.* 14¾ × 19⅞″

167. Push Button. *1981. Ink and wash. 14⅞ × 19⅞"*

168. Goya's Garden. 1981. Ink. 15 × 20"

170. Elf's Shoe. 1981. Ink and wash. 14¾ × 20"

169. Grid Fairy. 1981. Ink. 15 × 20"

171. Tree House. 1981. Ink. 14¾ × 20"

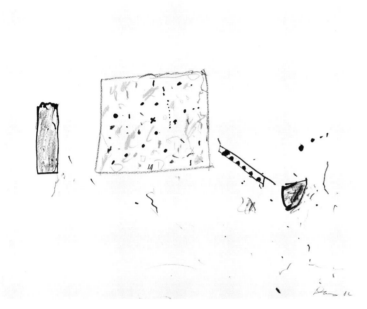

172. Play Ladder. *1982. Ink and crayon. 15 × 20"*

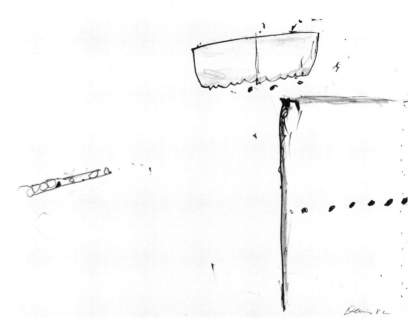

174. Flying Saucer. *1982. Ink and crayon. 15 × 20"*

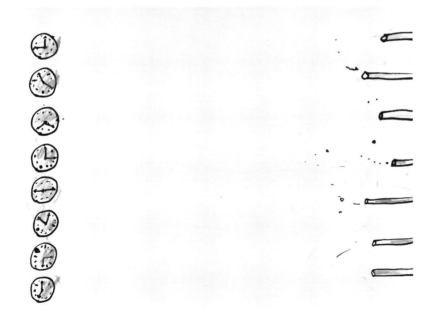

173. Time of Day. *1982. Ink and crayon. 15 × 20"*

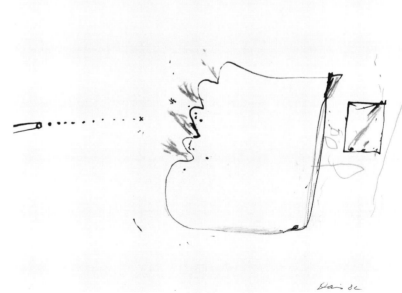

175. Target. *1982. Ink and crayon. 15 × 20"*

147

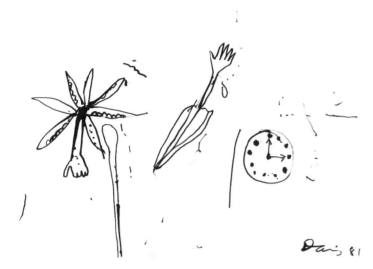

176. Help. *1981. Ink. 11 × 17"*

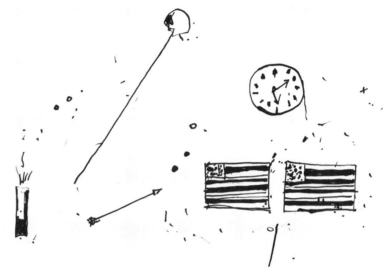

178. Two Flags. *1981. Ink. 11 × 17"*

177. Clock Watcher. *1981. Ink. 11 × 17"*

179. Davey Jones. *1981. Ink. 11 × 17"*

149

180. Encounter. *1980. Collage. 14 × 20″*

181. Visitor. *1981. Ink and crayon. 11 × 17"*

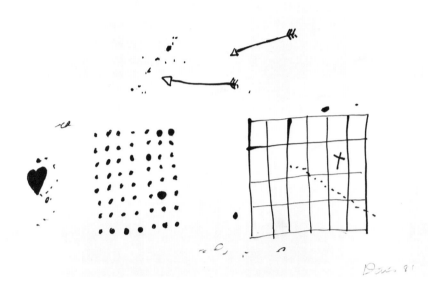

183. Heart and Cross. *1981. Ink. 11 × 17"*

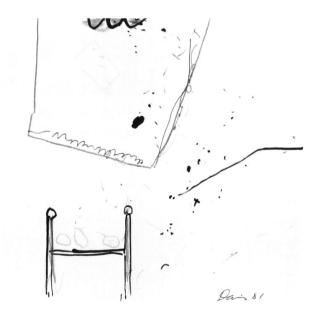

182. Enemy Bed. *1981. Ink and crayon. 11 × 17"*

184. Flowers. *1981. Ink and crayon. 11 × 17"*

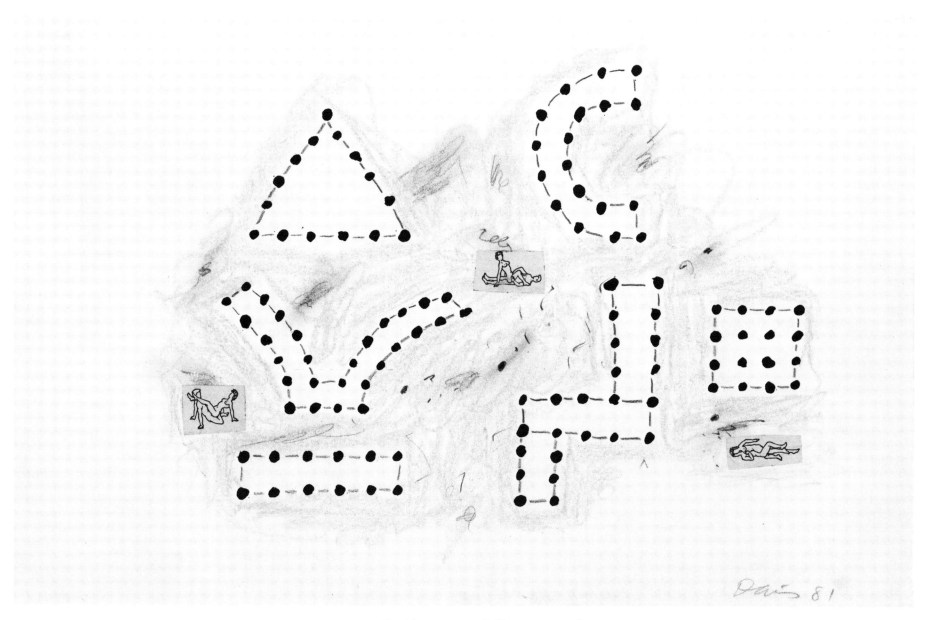

185. Positions. *1981. Collage. 11 × 17"*

186. Heads. 1982. Collage. 15 × 20″

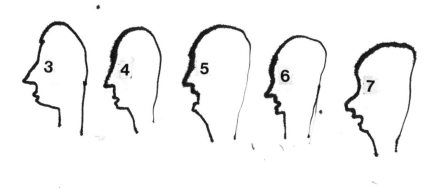

187. Five Heads. *1981. Collage.* 15 × 20″

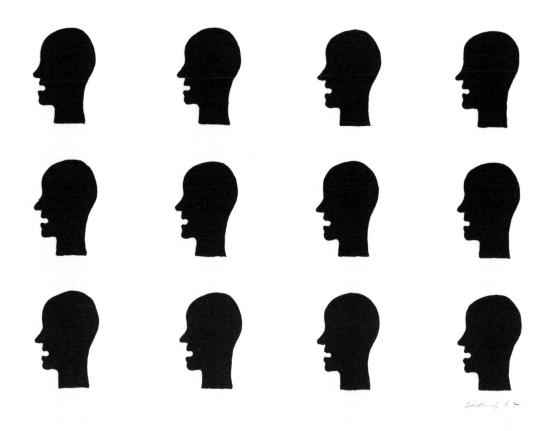

188. Self-Portraits. *1982*. Ink. *13½ × 16¼"*

189. Self–Portrait. *1982. Ink. 17⅝ × 15″*